RELIGION AND PHILOSOPHY FOR MODERN YOUTH

About the Author

Prof. J.N. Nanda, with a string of academic distinctions including two earned doctorates, multitude of awards from the IBC and American Biography Association, and other national and international awards, is a distinguished scientist, thinker and writer. He has represented India abroad many times. He has summarized his all embracing philosophy and religion as New Mahayana in which all 'isms' co-exist. Among his scientific contributions, mention can be made of his new light on the earth's internal structure, the origin of the moon and the origin of earth's magnetism etc. He has travelled practically in all continents and studied many languages. Besides his scientific books and publications, mention may be made of his book "Science and Technology in India's Transformation", released by the President of India at the Rashtrapati Bhawan in 1986. Other important books are *Foreign Policy of Co-existence—India*, *Glimpses of Indian History and Culture*, and *Co-operative Development of Marine Resources*.

RELIGION AND PHILOSOPHY FOR MODERN YOUTH

J.N. NANDA

CONCEPT PUBLISHING COMPANY, NEW DELHI-110059

ISBN 81-8069-013-X

First Published 2003

Published and Printed by
Ashok Kumar Mittal
Concept Publishing Company
A/15-16, Commercial Block, Mohan Garden
New Delhi-110059 (INDIA)

Phone : 25351460, 25351794
Fax : 091-11-25357103
Email : publishing@conceptpub.com

Preface

This little book contains the elixir of life for the human kind. The Nations of the World must be at peace. The United Nations can be strengthened to bring about respect for international law and thwart terrorism of every variety. The nations can compete for contributing to world prosperity and world culture. The internal and external peace can be assured through religious, economic and political coexisting policies. Science and technology can bring about sufficient production to meet the legitimate needs of all the people on this earth. Everyone has a share in the resources that are available.

There are sufficient grounds for all to see the dismal end of imperialism and fascism or of exploitation whether through captive markets or through captive populations. No country or people can assume any divine indulgence over others. Human mind has depths not fully fathomed and there is room for all kinds of beliefs and ambitions but need of the hour and of humanity is to guard against greed and self-indulgence at the cost of others. The whole world is in kinship to each other.

Indian secularism and New *Mahayana* are the key to peace and prosperity. The revolutions and momentous events grow out of seed strewn by thinkers and philosophers. This book, including the background of oriental and western philosophy, is towards the invention of new philosophy and understanding that can facilitate the knitting together of the world as one family. The new philosophy will use extensively science and scientific developments including experiments with genes, chemical and gene therapy to cure mankind from attraction of violence and injustice for private profit.

Throughout the ages, philosophy has ranked the highest and most certain through logic whetted by sharpest brains. But in the last couple of centuries, science has taken over all branches of knowledge. Modern science is the means of understanding the universe and is infinite in its reach. Philosophy is now left with inward interaction. It has still to concern itself with faith, transcendence, freedom, aesthetics and values as well as sundry ingredients of culture and all inputs for human happiness. Philosophy must continue to help nations as well as individuals in coping with the agony and ecstasy of existence.

Philosophy has to provide vision to pierce tradition and convention and from experiments with projection of thoughts and programmes provide numbers that can help us reject or modify these. Marcel (1949) regards humanity as lost in its chase of the salvation of its soul. The aim of the chase needs revision perhaps. We shall briefly go over the chronology of ideas and how there have been certain productive periods of creative ideas and then lean periods of commentaries often pedantic but unifying. The Chinese often hark back to legendary emperors who gave them original philosophy of Tao as well as social order before 3000 B.C. Later they love to draw inspiration again and again from Confucius or Lao Tze who laboured around the sixth century B.C. More than one strong emperor declared a particular philosophy as the official philosophy for their famous examinations searching for talent for becoming advisers to rulers. The strong emperors even loved to destroy creeds not following the officially selected philosophy. The Chinese defined and redefined their terms to include indigenous Taoist faith and Buddhist mysticism. They succeeded in formulating Cha'nism that spread as Zen to Japan and is now attracting adherents in Russia and India. The Chinese philosophy has had prolonged quiescent periods from the third to the sixth centuries A.D. and then from the finalization of new Confucianism in the eleventh century to the present. The philosophers there are groping for new goals after the laborious synthesis of all native and imported ideas. Salvation of material component and the spiritual component of the human being is now not the major concern but the Chinese philosopher is more concerned with stability of the society and the freedom that ought to be exercised by the individual in determining one's role in the affairs of the society. The Chinese have almost an uninterrupted weight of tradition and custom and have made almost a god of Confucius, an arch symbol of convention and manners. If a philosophy can integrate revolution with reaction, the Chinese philosophers might discover it.

One can easily see that the Indian philosophy has exhausted the creative drive when they reached *yoga* and *bhakti* or the filial devotion to the chosen god or a *guru* (preceptor). Indians have been more accommodating in taking up more than one philosophy ardently at the same time because of their fundamental belief in God approachable by many routes. Mysticism and *bhakti* are now reaching more people in the country along with the regard for modernization. The belief in reincarnation and ultimate ripening of seeds of *karma* in a succession of births is unshaken and has spread to all Indians. They had an important revolution when they uprooted superstitious belief in the efficacy of magic of incantations, "libations" and sacrifice of animals or materials valued by themselves for benefit of the gods or other beings. But now they have turned around and again extol miracles and miraculous favours through *bhakti* or through powers won and exercised howsoever reluctantly through *yoga*. Earlier only abodes of gods and places of pilgrimage were the sites of miracles favouring the moneyed clients. Now many men have come up claiming to be *yogis* and godmen with license from the Almighty to grant *diksha* i.e. accept new followers who can then receive favours from God. Society has to develop only by natural efforts of the citizens. If one were to depend on supernaturalism or on *kismet* then the ultimate responsibility is of no one and the world can merrily go on its own appointed course to the natural end in a black hole. The religious philosophers must invent a world-wide acceptance of some logical tests for miracles as this will clear the air for proper place to be given to spiritualism in human affairs. Spiritual life is still a question mark. It is about time that the Indian philosophy forget the ancient abusive terming of the Jain philosophy as atheistic and use it with results of scientific experiments bearing on the future of philosophy for globalisation. True globalisation can come only when there is a world federation with democratic constitution. In market development, there has to be accommodation for different levels of resources regarding education, training and welfare of women as well as children in different countries. A united world must work as a single family.

In this book we will have a look on the development of ideas on sundry philosophical subjects from various individuals and cultures. Philosophers in the west are more familiar with modern science and mathematics. Their use of new symbolic logic, thinking machines, numerical computer experiments, sensible deductions from prolific information and data foreshadows new creative developments in philosophy that can occur anywhere in the world due to explosion in information technology and access to intellectual developments anywhere. The creative philosophers will have to condense many lives into their single life to master relevant matter in philosophy, mathematics, physics, logic, *yoga* and fearless analysis with an eye on the practical aspects of their work in the pursuit of national and international goals. The western philosophy since Hegel is now become pedantic and is engaged in word splitting and often meaningless web of words and the sport of interpreting logical statements with diagrams, trying to improve on ancient systems of logic through diagrams. The mathematical theories of chaos are pretty much the parallel of Delphi technique to clothe the ideas of an author into philosophical acceptability.

Philosophy must consider the experience of people, the labours of scientists and earlier philosophers to arrive at a current verdict to be modified in the light of newer data in true style of science and leaning in Jain philosophy of scepticism mixed with own conclusions. We shall deal with conventional problems in philosophy in brief without any conclusive recommendations. Many problems have only been discussed by religion and metaphysics. And a grain of such conclusions need an ounce of faith for swallowing it, buts faith itself has grown out of curiosity and inner urge to invent explanations of intuitive or contrived answers to questions beyond reason. Human beings have an inherent curiosity and respect for questions like how and why. How did the world begin? How did human beings come into existence? What is the structure of thought etc.? Even illiterate tribals have myths about creation and the role of human beings in the universe. Faith grew out of the rational necessity of defining the first causes. Further, in this book, after a summary of chronological growth of philosophy, many distinct subjects of interest to the human beings are discussed. Feeling-based philosophy before Kant was replaced by reason-based one e.g. by Fichte, Schelling and Hegel. Fichte defined the movement in philosophy as thesis-anti-thesis and synthesis.

When the modern state is discussed, the situation in India is more in view. Similarly, modern religion is around current beliefs in India, besides the rest of the world. It has been noticed that an irreverent attitude stands in the way of western scholarship from understanding the Hindu view of life. In place of the actual content of *yoga* and meditation, the picture presented is of an indolent way of life. The priority even over treading the path of search for peace and fulfilment is on meritorious deeds and the ethical life as amplified in religious texts about the middle path and non-violence.

J.N. NANDA

Contents

1

Traditional Philosophy

CREATION

Primitive people everywhere had fanciful myths concerning the creation of the universe. It is only the modern science and the ancient Indian speculation that give the best approach. The modern idea is that the universe began as a result of one or more big bangs or exploding spots of energy. It is presumed that certain black hole becomes energetically unstable and explodes giving rise to emerging strings of galaxies. A galaxy later splits into stars and whole lot of heavenly bodies evolve from the stars or from concentration and dispersal of the starry material. The material gets concentrated at certain spots and thus planets are formed surrounding a star. The planets, in turn, explode to give satellites of the planets. Any remaining debris gives rise to meteors and shooting stars. Another contending scientific theory speculates that matter is continuously created at certain spots and also destroyed at some other spots. The big bang creation of the solar system occurred more than 9 billion years ago. The earth, an assembly of planetesimals attained full size practically 5 billion years ago and the moon formed on a scab explosively emitted from the earth about 4.2 billion years ago. The age of rocks picked up from the surface of the moon is 3.5 billion years but an older rock sample might be picked up or the time of the first atomic explosion in the innermost core of the earth might have been only 3.5 billion years ago.

The Indian myth speaks of the bursting of the *Brahma's* egg and thus the formation of the universe about 9 billion years ago. The astronomical distances and the ages are pretty much the same as the modern estimates. The ancient Hindus were well aware of the spherical shape of the earth and the central position of the sun in the solar system. But how about the Creator if any? Modern science does not recommend the belief or need of a creator. Just as the properties of matter determine the natural course and continuation of the universe, the same way, the creation or dissolution naturally come to pass. The Hindus believe the universe to be forever with repeated beginnings and endings in cyclic manner. The creation of a universe of composite materials was an argument for inferring the presence of a Creator, with the philosophers who followed the *Nyaya-Vaiseshaka* system of thought of ancient Hindus. The *Lokayats* or the materialists regard the formation of the universe as an accident and are certain that this calls for an eventual dissolution. The Indian atomists assign the creation to the nature of atoms practically like the modern scientists. Kumaril Bhat (eighth century A.D.) denied the belief in creation or dissolution. He held to a constant process of becoming and passing away. The Chinese do not believe in a creator, but their philosophy explains creation or dissolution to follow a philosophic understanding of the terms 'being and not being'. Universe is coeval with time and its non-existence at any time is beyond imagination. The Tao is undefinable and so it leads in a subtle manner to creation of shapes and to even conscious creatures through the inter-play of Chi and Li, the equivalents of stuff and format.

GOD

Many religions and philosophies allow a creator but most do not harbour a constant controller and regulator. Hindus have *Brahma* as the creator. Christians have God and Muslims call Him Allah. God is imagined in the style of a despotic king who can interfere and regulate at all times. The non-regulating God prefers to will the laws of nature and retribution or of cause and effect that run the universe. God, according to *Ishopnishad* (Vedic composition around 1500 B.C.), is present everywhere and active in His creative ways. He is immanent. Human beings are supposed to discriminate between good and evil. According to Aristotle, God of religious belief could not be totally perfect since He had to create the universe in order to become Himself. This would support the *Jain* view that the universe has always been there, sometimes in expanded form and sometimes shrunk to a point. The creator may be called the energy that is the unmoved mover.

In general, the view is that God as Creator or Controller does not exist. God is the creation of man in his own image. Since man hankers after joy. The God he has created is joy, consciousness and truth. God can be the sum total of all godly qualities. The evolution of the capacity to simulate resulted in consciousness. Religion, however, claims that consciousness has an objective reality. Perhaps, the cooperative action of all minds is God.

The Hindus regard *Brahma* as the creator and the religions of Jewish origin call him God or Allah. *Brahma* or the non-regulating type prefers to will the presence of laws of nature and laws of retribution or cause and effect that run the universe. He has made rules that govern the destiny of human beings according to their actions. The human beings are permitted discrimination between good and evil but they are also surrounded by aberrations like greed and anger as well as *avidya* or false knowledge. Aristotle (third century B.C.) had a proposal to offer. According to him, God of religious belief could not be perfect if he would also be the creator since a creator has to create to be complete. The Jain view is that the universe is always there sometimes in expanded form and sometimes shrunk to zero. The Creator may be energy that is the unmoved mover. The Buddha (sixth century B.C.) was quite clear that the presence or the absence of a creator made little difference to human happiness since human beings have to work out their own salvation and cannot depend on any grant of favour. The Chinese philosophers were also concerned with human welfare than in empty metaphysical explanation even when they permitted belief in myths of creation and the dispensation of heaven in human affairs.

Nagarjuna (250 A.D.) argued for philosophical nihilism finding realism only in the void of space. So many theories of creation start with properties of space or ether. The *Mimansaks* believed in creation and dissolution but Udyan argued against the *Mimansaks* and believed in God.

During the mind set for French Revolution, the belief in God was considered bound with submission to autocracy. Rousseau fought the establishment's materialism and atheism. According to him, the goal for man is to achieve perfection and to bring happiness to others. Duty must supersede beauty and morality must receive prior attention than happiness. Shankar believed in singular *Brahma* while Ramanuja reasoned in favour of pluralistic *Brahma*. Universal theism was offset by the cult of *Shaktism* (i.e. practically necromancy).

Through *yoga*, transmigration of soul can be seen by remembrance of past lives. But belief is not enough, one has to exert to be god-like through morality. Aurobindo Ghosh (1872-1950) declared in his 'Life Divine' that mystic consciousness is open to all.

Descartes regards God as infinite in every way; Anselm regards Him as perfect and Hegel's God is Absolute. Kant invested God with regulatory power over reason. In modern times, William James regards God as pragmatic Reality. The chief argument for human freedom is that determinism will make non-sense of moral responsibility. Surrender of all deeds to a personal God does not free one from responsibility for one's deeds or give an escape from bearing the results of one's *karma*. The surrender can only bring easy acceptance of results. Cultivation of scientific reasoning alone can dispel confusion.

WHAT AM I ?

Identity of self is an important philosophical question. Most people, including atheists, have come to believe that a sentient being has a soul, especially a human being. It is also practically universal belief that the soul is everlasting. Religions of Indian origin believe in the transmigration of soul at every rebirth. The religions of Jewish origin teach that the souls after the death of the live body last in heaven or hell till eternity as judged on the judgement day by the Almighty depending on the way the soul used the all too unique human life granted to it. The Indian philosophers argue that since there is no appeal, the God's whim should not prevail, but every soul that is destined for hell be given another chance and that is why the rebirth is logical. Even stay in heaven till eternity will diminish in charm rather soon. Acharya Rajneesh and some modern thinkers propound that the soul is coterminous with the body that it is endowed with at every birth. The sum total of actions in that or previous births has already determined the initial conditions for the next birth at the moment of expiry of each life span and so no entity called soul has to pass from one body to the next. The religions have without their acknowledgement heavily relied on the ancient Egyptian philosophy about the soul and its journey after death to the judgement seat and beyond. They regarded certain distant planets as temporary resting stations for departed souls. There is picturesque detail of the travels of the departed soul in Egyptian mythology and practically the same version is recorded in the Hindu *Puranas*.

The belief in rebirth or the judgement day has been a good policeman for all societies. In primitive societies the social punishment was a sufficient deterrent. The Sikhs of India believe that the voice of God will issue from the unanimous decision of any five Sikhs in the brotherhood. The Chinese as well as the modern atheists give due regard and are prepared to submit to the village council but this is because they are not so fond of regular police and courts in the country. In the U.S.A. the courts have due regard to the law as well as public opinion.

An individual is thus a soul besides the body, but the individual has a personality of his own, an ego, a set of values, an active brain that is ready to play with logic and try all avenues in self interest. The philosophers point out the harm that ego and care for face can cause to the individual. They promise certain success and happiness if one can shed the ego and learn the benefits of mildness and submission. On the other hand, great deeds have been accomplished by men with ambition and ego. One cannot but point out that all results are not what one expects from his or her work. The results should better be not dwelt upon before or after. In the pursuit of happiness logic, can be the first casualty. The spirit of acceptance must be embraced after doing one's duty or self-imposed task. This can be done in the theist formula "Thy will must prevail" or the super egoist formula "I am one with God or the Universe and so master of all that befalls me." This is also the *Vedantic* teaching which one reaches only after first mastering one's ego !

EPICURUS, CHARUVAK AND THEIR BRAND OF MATERIALISM

Epicurus of Athens or *Charuvak* of India of the Vedic age were gross materialists denying the interest of God or gods in human affairs. They held that pursuit of pleasure is the be all and end all of human life. Epicurus railed against marriage since it confers unnecessary worry and responsibility. Beliefs that belittle human beings must be un-welcome. He also gave the recipe of acceptance and submission to escape pain. (The saints and religious martyrs made foolish sacrifices). *Charuvak* questioned the practice of supplicating or demeaning oneself before God or gods. God, gods and soul do not exist. It is the senses that are important and one feels pain or pleasure as encountered by the senses. He logically opposed all magic, astrology and divination. Epicurus was hero-worshipped by the Greek poet Lucretius (99-55 B.C.) and his poem on Epicurus has been extolled by Shelley. The poet feels that when religion has ground man into dust, it is Epicurus who has raised him back on to the human pedestal. He vanquished religion of superstitious fear and vain hope. Whenever in the west there was vehement opposition to oppressive religion, people have been turning to Epicurus, as in the eighteenth century England of Benthem. *Charuvak* had tough luck, the youths of aristocratic families were always attracted but they had to practise it as members of secret brotherhoods. *Charuvak* was condemned by both theistic and atheistic religions since it was rebellion against the pillars of true faiths of ascetic virtue and belief in retribution, cause and effect or rebirth. The clergies of all faiths abhorred Epicurus or *Charuvak*. Invariably the practical but rare instances of success of faith in incantations and pilgrimages won over logic of *Charuvak* or Epicurus.

STOICISM, ZENO

How to deal with misfortunes. The Christians regard misfortunes as tests of faith imposed by God and one has to successfully cross them in faith. Hindus regard these as punishment for misdeeds already counted against them from this or past lives and so have no legitimate grouse against such happenings which seem to be most undeserved and should be countered by better performance still, to compensate for past misdeeds and the automatic computer of destiny will liberate one from misfortune when the account is squared. To bear with misfortune in quiet surrender is the way of the devotees of God or Guru who may cancel the debit account if he is satisfied with the devotion currently displayed. Some of lofty morals and supreme confidence in their own actions endure misfortune with a smile. These are the stoics, first articulated by Zeno, the Greek and practised so thoroughly by brave men everywhere notably by the Rajputs of India and chivalrous knights of Europe. The Rajputs held it a duty to give shelter to a supplicant. There are instances when they gave shelter to rebels of the emperor and took on themselves to sacrifice everything to see the rebel reach his friends and escape the emperor's wrath. The Chinese have a culture of self respect or "no blemish on their face" and have gladly suffered diplomatic or other reverses than allow the face to suffer. Stoics will suffer for their word and share their means and bear all hardships for a cause not theirs, but made their own in a selfless way. On this account the Rajputs of Rajasthan have proven to be stoics. The women of the world have been stoics all along and their stoicism is only now being recognised when the politicians are out to give them old-age pensions and a share in political power.

The fire walkers in ecstasy are stoics of a kind. Marcus Aureleus, the Roman emperor and a successful campaigner was a keen stoic. He believed the entire universe to be single entity and an individual's misfortune was being shared by the whole universe, which should sufficiently make him resign to it. He recommended love for those particularly who do one harm. He anticipated Mahatma Gandhi. Kant's ethical system in the eighteenth century was close to that of the stoics. Stoics practised equality before the law. Confucius was a great believer in the same. He advocated Chang (i.e. do to others as you wish to be done to you) and Shu (i.e. do not do to others that you do not wish to be done to you). He had forestalled Jesus by many centuries in this. These stoic statements do not rest on any faith in God but only on humanism or human nature as believed by Confucius. A stoic does his duty or takes action irrespective of expectation of success. Krishna in his *Gita* exhorts action to be undertaken as one's allotted or chosen duty and necessarily as dedicated to the deity and nothing else. The Jains have developed a frame of mind that always regards results of actions as uncertain being influenced by many extraneous factors not considered by the person or beyond his ken and calculation. The Chinese acceptance of Ming is a way of accepting determinism and inevitability of the world as it unfolds.

MAGIC, RITUALS AND MIRACLES

Religion now means worship, love and service to humanity. For primitive people it was assurance of help from God or gods who were won by humility and obedience to elders or the recognised guides in invoking god's favour or by gifts and sacrifice in the name of the God. Religious ecstasy was experienced through singing, intoxicating drinks or through dancing solo or in a group. The goal of peace and good life came much later. All wishes and desires were supposed to be met by magical charms and the purchased goodwill of the priests and sundry holy men. The *Vedas* composed about five thousand years ago in the very infancy of civilised life were primarily magical *mantras* or poetic compositions which were to be recited along with sacrificial offerings to gods. The first offering was made to fire for reaching the god and later the offering was to be shared among all those present, besides paying a separate fee to the priest officiating at the sacrifice. The belief was that the magical fruit of the sacrifice and ritual will reach the beneficiary suddenly at some time in the future. There would be gullible people who would like to have the fruit quickly and bribe the priests in that belief. The magical fruition of wishes was put to ridicule by the Buddha when he castigated desires as well as supernatural interference in the fulfilment of human wishes. The *Gita* endorsed the uncertainty of results of any action including sacrifices.

Assurance of heaven through gifts to priests was widespread in the middle ages and Protestantism railed against such practice of the Popish priests. Around the time of the Buddha, the Hindus were prone to make spectacles of animal sacrifice for winning God's favour. The common people were harassed no end by the costly rituals. People engaged less in genuine effort than in spending money on costly rituals for miraculous satisfaction of their desires. Even as late as couple of decades ago, the whole Hindu world was agog with rumours about idols of Ganesha drinking milk ! Miracles are customarily associated with sacred relics, temples, idols, graves, and now-a-days godmen and *pirs* or their *samadhis* and *stupas*, and their personal memorabilia, etc. The modern cinema, which can depict all miracles on the screen, has specialised in mythological movies and showing miracles on the screen and has strengthened superstition no end. Many are now counting on their turn to benefit from some miracle or the other as the human ability can ignore many failures and build up on a rare success possibly by fluke. Certain occurrences are uncannily probable miraculous happenings but a positive verdict would require scrutiny by magicians and more honest observers armed with statistics and extensive data.

KISMET

Human beings are rational and look to cause and effect relationships. Universe is the most complex and intricate occurrence. How did it all begin is shrouded in mystery. Where does the arrow of time point ? Only the poet would know whether the world will end in fire or in cold inertia. Modern physics endorses that uncertainty is an essential element in the existence of even the elementary particles. Prediction is impossible even few steps ahead. Due to multiple connections in the universe there are many sequences of events existing at the same time and any happening is a result of multiple sequences focused on that instant in space and time. Even the distinction of cause and effect gets blurred due to mixing of spatial elements with time. For giving a sop to our minds looking for cause and effect, the idea of God was invented as a supreme doer. In order to explain the uneven initial conditions of human beings the theory of *karma* or retribution from past births of an everexisting but reincarnating soul was invented. None of this can be universally valid if one also has to expect justice and kindness from God. Simplest would be to extend the significance of modern scientific conclusions and give up insistence on cause and effect. The happenings happen because these have been inexplicably and inescapably fated to happen. This is, in nutshell, the *Kismet* often trotted out as a palliative to human suffering or for necessary leakage of inflated ego.

The Islamic explanation of uneven and sometimes downright injustice of fate is rather simple. God is not only the supreme doer, but he is also the supreme autocrat with no limitations outside his own nature. He is very kind and those that throw themselves in his camp and hope for his kindness, receive it. He can pluck them out of even the stream destined for hell. Simplest escape was offered by the Hindu view of accepting what happens and feel all the time that God is on their side. The Indian view is for self help to avoid pitfalls and to do one's duty without expectation of expected results since there were innumerable variables affecting the course of events. Man thinks logically and he would assume that *Kismet* must also be framed by God or one of the gods and would it be possible to influence God by prayer to escape troublesome fate. Many self appointed god's agents sprang up to prey on the misgivings of people regarding their *Kismet*. There grew cults and sanctuaries, flowing rivers, rocks and springs where one could have his wishes fulfilled. Many temples, shrines and *dargahs* or tombs, sport visible symbols of wishes fulfilled. There was also a great eagerness to learn about future events and one paid fees to soothsayers and learned divines for a peep into their future. The age-old lore of superstition, skills of horoscope casting became popular. Forecasting is most of the time pure guesswork plus some ability of the mind to recognise faint signals from the future. Such signals are now easy to understand when we know that electron wave functions which govern the probability of its occurrence, are continuous in space and time. It is best to steer clear from knowledge of the future. Since the knowledge can only be very approximate and could mislead you into attempting to fend it off or to modify your natural actions in efforts to modify the believed future. Such attempts can lead to a different future which may be even more disagreeable or the future is not affected which also means wasted efforts.

There are innumerable churches, temples and tombs, where the custodians spread the account of the shrine assuring the fulfilment of one's wishes as expressed in prayers there. This is also a statistical magic. Failures are forgotten and lone successes are tom-tomed no end like the grant of a son to emperor Akbar by the pilgrimage to Ajmer. There is never any need to interfere with destiny. The destined calamities have fallen to the lot of greatest divines and devotees alike. Without regard to any prior knowledge of destiny, one can persist in betterment of one's conditions and struggle and hope for the best and be prepared to accept as the destiny unfolds which according to all account is inescapable, any way. The Hindu *jap*, *tapa* and *mantra*, or their equivalent among the Christians and Muslims or the Sikhs and self-control of the Jains and the Jews may be beneficial intrinsically but can have no direct influence on the destined happenings. The soul and its continuity should be recognised for what it is, a rationalisation of the world but not of any physical impact on the happenings in the world.

There are certain well-known recipes, however, to stay at peace with the *Kismet*. Mostly, it is held that persistent prayers help one to accept what happens and to be equally unaffected by the momentary victories and defeats. Faith and prayers generate stability. Conviction as of the agnostics and general assurance of being helpful and thankful to all mankind can also make one live and die in poise as happened to Socrates. Gandhi desired everyone to choose his actions carefully after due deliberation and self confidence and God will give him the strength and ability to bear the consequences.

BRAHMCHARYA

Brahmcharya stands for both the first preparatory stage of human life on the average extending to 25 years of age and also for the training for self-control particularly the control of sexual desires and general obedience to rules of conduct (for an aspirant) known as *yama* and *niyam* : *Yama* is control of senses of sight, hearing, feeling and taste. *Niyam* is rules of conduct and behaviour to parents, teachers and fellow human beings. Followers of *yama* and *niyam* are *brahmcharis* and reach success as students, aspirants and virtuous folk. A *brahmchari* is prepared for the life's remaining stages of *grihasth* (family man from age 25 to age 50 years), *vana prastha* (life of detachment with respect to personal property and family) and spending more time for public service without any selfish motive while sometimes staying in the family home and sometimes staying away from home with learned people and instructors in meditation etc. between the age 50 to 75 years; and finally *sanyas* or away from mundane concerns, devoting most of the time to meditation, religious devotions and service of the people (age 75 onwards).

According to Indian philosophy, the purpose of life is to rise above *maya* or illusion of sense assessed world as real, and to realise the presence of God or supreme arbiter within oneself. This would confer everlasting bliss and oneness with the universe and all living beings. *Brahmcharya* is the essential first step on the ladder for this climb. From another angle too, from the ever-present lust for and crime against women, the welfare of both men and women demands self control by human beings. There is present throughout human history predilection to loose morals and denigration of women. Women as a gender were regarded as sinful and seductive as well as an invitation to sin. Ancient seers as well as modern reformers like Dayananda, Mahatma Gandhi and Satya Sai Baba emphasise *brahmcharya* as a proper vow to overcome the misfortunes of ill-health, overpopulation and poverty. *Brahmcharya* is the fit identity of the man for his formative first twenty-five years. It is also a necessary *yama* (discipline) for whole life in the pursuit of human perfection. Stolen sex, adultery, child abuse, unnatural vice have been prevalent throughout the ages and more attempt to practise *Brahmcharya* is indicated. The literature is full of homosexuality indulged in by the Greeks, Egyptians, Romans, etc. But the eastern people including Indians are no better. At Khajuraho, there is permanent record in stone of sexual exploits of men including sex with animals. Indian teaching is not for suppression of sex but for self control and sublimation of sex. Even relative freedom of mixing of sexes in play and dance is respectfully entertained in the cult of Krishna and the Gopis. The age-old concepts of revelry at Holi and fun and frolic in mixed gatherings as well as all–inclusive hospitality to strangers have worked against prudery. The other extreme step against loose morals was taken by Islam that of segregation of sexes and confining women to *purdah* and strict subservience to men but this has led to psychological imbalance in society and could be at the root of Muslim *Jehad* and love of violence or cultivation of group hate for all kinds of infidels. This cannot be the elixir for a multi-community state as India or most of the world. Let us see what success the Taliban achieve in their conversion of human beings in Afghanistan to cattle.

Brahmcharya, in nutshell, describes the right path for a student or an aspirant. It stands for rigorous self control, sublimation of sex and self-confidence with absence of guilt feelings. *Brahmcharya* includes injunctions against gambling, another evil of civilisation. *Smriti Sutras* condemn also wine.

REALITY

Thinkers and philosophers have been attempting to grasp reality for ages. Science has shed some light on the complexity of the subject. Mechanistic logic, cause and effect relationship, arrows of time and space are now known to be valid only under certain limitations, beyond which they give way to random occurrences, probabilistic outcomes and fuzziness in time and space. This prepares us better to approach the subject of reality. Upto a limited extent the Charuvakian certainty of the senses is sufficient. Full faith in the mentor or the *guru* and following the laid down rituals can be enough for the smooth living of an average person. When the rules of reason are found inadequate, a probing mind tries to dig deeper into reality. Human nature is no longer restricted to self preservation of the beasts but its true quality is named by the ancients "*Manav Dharama*" or humanism. This covers also altruism, self sacrifice, social justice and devotion to family as well as the tribe or all mankind.

Scientific explanations are never static, a well-documented and believable theory today may be found incorrect tomorrow. Human reason usually trails behind human understanding. When causes and effects were regarded uniquely related, the simplest view of the universe was a creation of God, the creator, preserver and destroyer. Reason also required negation of "good" and so were devil, the *Shani* mischief, and myriads of catastrophies explained away. All this could inculcate patience and survivability in human beings. The logic of cause and effect, given the vicissitudes of fortune of the newly born, led to the theory of rebirth, of *karma* and the Indian doctrines of *sansar* and *sanskar* that attach to the soul in its transmigration. The beliefs in God, soul, and reaping the results of past deeds in the same or the after life are all consistent logic but these do not constitute reality. The religious beliefs are for the consolation of human beings and if they give them hope and peace at the time of death, so be it. Many religions believe in an everlasting life in heaven or hell after the brief chance of living on earth. Astronomers are certain that there is no heaven in the universe, but there can be many candidates for hell since the form of life after death is unknown. Divine dispensation may strike an ordinary mortal as unjust. The apologists only call it a test from the most high or a proof of the omnipotence of gods who need not be circumscribed by any rules discovered by human beings. Who are we to question His rulings, given the vast canvas of past, present and future only known to him. The all too mundane assurance of salvation by rituals, incantations, and mediation by saints, *pirs*, holy men, tantrists or through *bhakti* and grace, proceed from the quality of love and affection inherent in God. This kind of projection of reality is so dear to the priests and gate-keepers of all religions, being their bread and butter. The *Gita* faces this problem by its exhortation that one can only perform an action and not dwell on a pre-determined result accruing to him. Results are not fully determined by one's own actions but are influenced by many other variables which are uncertain. For the pious, a simple rule is to perform all actions as dedicated to one's existence. Even scientific efforts illustrate this. Galileo fortunately was vindicated, many years after his discoveries. The scientists and philosophers of his day only punished him for his audacity of stating truth that could not be recognised by self-opinionated peers. This happens all the time.

Today, when matter and energy, space and time are merging into each other in the flights of theory, mind and matter remain separated as two banks of a river. Acharya Rajnish is one of the moderns squarely facing the dilemma. He regards body and soul to be co-existent and co-terminating. He admits of transmigration of souls but is silent about the nature of soul when parted from the last body, like the virtual photons of modern physics. Theistic thought assigns an objective reality to consciousness, calling it God, or Cosmic Mind, or the Living Silence etc. It carries some conviction because of the examples when we find human mind to respond to signals from other human brains or from matter or events past or future. This may be entirely due to the unknown biophysics of multiplex-connected system of particles in the human brain. We thus revert to the New *Mahayana* of simultaneous belief in many ideas.

When logical deduction fails, one may resort to analogies that may help the understanding but can convince none. Each individual is like a bubble on the surface of the vast sea of existence. It is not heralded by any fanfare in the manner just of a transitory bubble and it vanishes without trace. Or we are the dream actors in the dream universe of God and so we must ignore any pain or pleasure that comes our way in the dream of God. Such analogies are deceptions that smother deeper enquiry. The basic social need is to accept the desirability of being good and neighbourly and make this acceptance free from all props of religion primarily because religions apparently differ and in place of uniting people often separate them into US and THEM. It is for this reason that there was the invention of *Mahayana* in the times of the Buddhist heyday which spread all over the world uniting all the known gods and goddesses in the success of prayers as well as keeping the path of right action and individual efforts for own salvation. Today also there is need for equal solicitude for all religious striving, and the theories of mixed economy and coexistence of various political machines served by democracy and care for human rights.

Good and evil arise from the overriding interest in self-advancement. We have to feel our personality expanded to accommodate others. This is the basis of all cultures. Saints also lay stress on pious deeds along with love for others. Life becomes well ordered, only if one can hold to an aim in life. For some it is service of others or for the resurgence of society. A large number of gifted people find satisfaction in creative activity. Any work carried out with devotion can be completed in a creative fashion. The work of painters, sculptors, poets, composers and scientists is the pinnacle of culture and civilisation. Modern poets and composers are meaningfully enriching the life of many in the world today. Scientists pursue their objectives holding on to truth and objectivity. They have no place for any fundamentalism. The scientific theories are always tentative and are immediately discarded or revised in the light of fresh observations or new data. Scientific results have to be checkable and reproducible as well as conducive to cover an ever wider range of experience. Scientific approach is an assured way to healthy thought and is being diligently embraced by all developing societies.

Human beings have evolved from blind and prolific creation. The direction of evolution is refinement and the propagation of genes. Human population has reached a saturation point for existing resources and technology. The urgent need is to refine the human gene to root out violence and arrogance. So that there is no further threat of war which may destroy the whole civilisation. Pursuit of happiness without jostling others, will automatically result in continuous improvement of society. The only relevant questions about reality are about our part in society and recognition of purpose of one's life. Secularism is the philosophy of acceptance and coexistence that comes to terms with reality. Secularism does not renounce religion but it embraces all religions which it seeks to reform.

2

Chronology Pertaining to Philosophy

2500 B.C.	Chinese Emperor, First Taoist – Fu Hsi
2000 B.C.	Vedic Period in north India. Also Brihaspati (leading Hedonist).
1500 B.C.	Vyasa, the composer of *Mahabharata*, Krishna, the charioteer hero of *Mahabharata* and the instructor of *Bhagwad Gita*, complete philosophy within the epic poem *Mahabharata*.
1100 B.C.	Gautam Rishi, the legendary composer of *Nyaya Sutra*.
700 B.C.	Kapila Rishi: the legendary composer of *Sankhya Shastra*
651 B.C. to 479 B.C.	Confucius: humanness, righteousness, prosperity and wisdom.
Between 1000 B.C. and 200 B.C.	Badrayna – *Brahm Sutra.*
598 B.C. to 527 B.C.	Mahavira, 24th Jain Tirthankar.
563 B.C. to 483 B.C.	Gautam Buddha: Banish desire and kill *karma* and escape rebirth. Follow right path or the middle path, right action and renunciation.
450 B.C. to 250 B.C.	*Dhampada*, Theravada Buddhism.
1500 B.C. to 1000 A.D.	*Puranas*: Hindu myths and religious discourses.
Between 1200 B.C. and 200 A.D.	*Manusmriti*: ancient law book of the Hindus.
d. 399 B.C.	Socrates: virtue and knowledge gc

	together.
384 B.C. to 322 B.C.	Aristotle: Soul as the sum of the powers and processes of the organism.
371 B.C. to 289 B.C.	Mencius, Philosophical Taoism of Lao Tze (about 400 B.C.).
300 B.C. to 50 B.C.	Miscellaneous Jain *Sutras*.
273 B.C. to 232 B.C.	Ashoka: Propagates Buddhism around 250 B.C.
	Kannada Rishi – Vaiseshaka Philosophy.
Between 250 B.C. and 350 A.D.	Patanjali Rishi – Yoga Sutra.
1 A.D. to 34 A.D.	Jesus Christ.
50 A.D.	*Mahayana* Buddhism.
526 A.D.	Bodhidharma in China.
638 A.D. to 713 A.D.	Hui Neng teaches Zen or Cha'nism.
220 A.D.	Collapse of Han Dynasty and dark age of philosophy in China until the advent of New Taoism in the sixth century A.D.
618 A.D. to 906 A.D.	Neo Confucianism, Golden Age in China, Tang Dynasty.
668 A.D. to 844 A.D.	Study of Tao (Truth).
500 A.D. to 1400 A.D.	*Tantra* in Buddhism and Hinduism.
800 A.D.	Shankara.
850 A.D.	Gunbhadra, Jain Philosopher.
1100 A.D.	Neo Confucianism trusts Chi and Li to be the basic structure of the universe or stuff and principle respectively.
1130 A.D. to 1200 A.D.	Chu Hsi : All people are my brothers and sisters.
1200 A.D.	Madhava (Vedantist Philosopher).
1500 A.D. to 1600 A.D.	Kabir, Guru Nanak.
1560 A.D. to 1605 A.D.	Akbar, the Great. Secularism as State Policy.
1641 A.D. to 1727 A.D.	Newton. Gravitation, scientific method.
1637 A.D.	Descartes: Father of philosophy, intellectualism and optimism . . . .
1774 A.D. to 1804 A.D.	Kant: We have duties as well as rights. Choice is also determined by mind and

	temperament. He placed religion within bounds of pure reason.
Voltaire	Religion rests in worship and justice.
Rousseau	Only that part of history has value that has contemporary significance.
1817 A.D.	Hegel: Laws of thought.
1836 A.D. to 1886 A.D.	Shri Rama Krishna All faiths lead to same God.
1859 A.D.	Publication of 'origin of species' by Darwin.
1861 A.D. to 1941 A.D.	Tagore. Unity of learning, Aesthetics.
1869 A.D. to 1948 A.D.	Gandhi, Civil Disobedience used in revolutionary struggle (Thoreau). Nietzsche and Schopenhauer.
1933 A.D.	Realism is pragmatically justified, Cosmic Mind acceptance leads to chance and faith.
1907 A.D.	Jean Paul Sartre: Existentialism with atheistic belief.
	Contemporary Indian Mysticism: Vivekananda, Aurobindo Ghosh, J. Krishnamurthy.
1949 A.D.	Subjective Idealism is against the touchstone of experience.
	Objective idealism retains reality as rational.
	Idealism includes Berkeley's theism
1956 A.D.	Ernst Nagel: Naturalism in Logic without metaphysics.
1968 A.D.	Paul Kurtz: Progress in humanism means freeing of moral values from dogma. Ideas must conform to present needs and social demands.

3

Basics of Religion

The basics of religion include worship, theories of creation, deity and prayer, priest-craft, religious obligations and virtuous life. Mysticism and spiritual experiences are often coloured by religious beliefs but are not confined to a specific religion.

WORSHIP

Worship is a common factor in all religions. The primitive man moved in a family group or at most in his tribe constituted of few families. The poets among them invented myths to satisfy their questioning minds. There would be happier or sad days almost at random as if some superior force was happy or angry with them. This led to the invention of all kinds of gods almost in a parallel hierarchy to the tribe. They reasoned to influence the gods to assist them or to desist from harming them. This led to vows and sacrifices or feeding of sacred fires and to place votive offerings. Soon the tribes had medicine men who presided over such sacrifice routines and claimed special mental or verbal connection with some god or the other. Recitation of qualities and deeds of the god, singing praises of the gods, offerings and sacrifices to the gods became communal or individual worship. Special occasion brought worship festivals.

When people discovered strange capacities of the human mind through the use of intoxicants, fasts, self-hypnosis and intense faith, their use was emphasized. Light and music were considered divine gifts and these became prominent in worship along with use of incense and flowers. From the consideration of peace among the worshippers of different gods, either one of the gods was exalted from among different gods as a king was exalted among the people, or various gods were regarded as manifestations of the same One God. Greeks, Romans, Jews, Christians and Muslims adopted one way, the Buddhists and the Hindus adopted the other way. It was natural for the Hindus to discover unity in diversity and invent *Mahayana* and now New *Mahayana*. Any person should be allowed in comfort to worship his own chosen deity and there is little pressure for conformism. Such an attitude permitted the Hindus to embrace and absorb all kinds of religion, gods and modes of worship.

According to the Hindus, God is present everywhere for all times. Saints like Kabir and Nanak exhort the seeker to find Him within oneself. They seek salvation through moral life devoted to doing good to others, through charity and kinship with all. The Hindu and Sikh prayer ends with the wish for the universal welfare. They also teach easy steps for meditation and reaching *samadhi* or a state when one feels attuned to the universe. Everyone can follow this route where the first signpost is the hearing of the omnipresent sound and seeing a light by the mind's eye. This led to the use of bells or conch shells or lighted candles in the worship of idols or *sakar* gods. At start whether at the primitive stone-henge type altars in U.K. or the sacrifice of a lamb, horse or an ox elsewhere, the concept was to seek godly favour as one attempted to seek from worldly despots, by sacrificing one's best for them or in their name. Abraham attempted to sacrifice his son in that line. The sacrifice of animals or men was later replaced by parting with food, coins or flowers in the name of the deity. For many Hindus or Muslims or others, worship meant brief encounter with the idol, the sacred tomb or relic or the holy book and receiving a sweet named God's favour. This was a good way to trap children into sacred visiting. The Hindus, particularly the Jains, had a theory that all indulgence, and selfish care is irreligious. Self denial, vows of self chastisement, standing on one leg, etc. seemed to make worship real and intense. This kind of aberration was very much evident among the Hindus in the days of the Buddha who himself belonged to such a fraternity before his own intense wish to succeed convinced him that the preferred middle path was not the path of self torture. The prevalent social pastime is communal singing of hymns in praise of deity and partaking of the sweet or meal at the end of the prayer meeting. There are so many fasts and festivals for family and for public participation. A worship including the eating and the drinking of god himself is symbolic magic. The ancient Aryans named the liquor *Soma* as a god. In *Shakta* worship, even today, serving meat and liquor is considered necessary. Ancestor worship is almost universal. The feeding of the Brahmins on special days is also part of ancestor worship. Modern science has brought it home that every one is a continuation of the ancestral gene thereby invoking the importance of ancestors. The Hindus found merit in being worshipful and rarely criticised the object being worshipped. Lord Krishna, in His *Gita* declaimed that the recipient of all oblations was God Himself, to whomsoever such offerings were made. The worship of certain plants, trees, snakes and stones, rivers and mountains were all popular. All tombs, *samadhis*, or *stupas* are fair objects for sacred glimpse or *darshan* as are holy men and recluses. The devotees regard idols as only the communication channels to One God. Indian Muslims since Akbar's time are aware of this significance and on the whole tolerate the idol worship of the Hindus. Prayer, charity and meditation are additional ingredients of worship.

The Hindus regard the cow as a scared animal and will not, therefore, kill it for food. The Muslims echo the hatred of the Jews for pork and will not eat pig's meat. It is interesting to delve deep into history and understand the true significance of religious regard for the cow of the Hindus and the hatred of pork of the Muslims. The word for the cow and the *Vedic* couplets is the same and by linguistic transfer "cow", the animal became sacred. The sacredness increased when it was found to be close to Krishna, the divine cow-herd. Cow also could be the simplest symbol for protection by the agriculturist population of India and greater India from the onslaught of the barbarians to the west and north who herded horses and sheep and not so much the cows. The hatred of pork stems from the ancient hatred of the Jews for the Greeks who celebrated their victories over the cities of the Jewish country by offering burnt offerings of pork to their gods. The Thai entrants, who colonised parts of Assam in India, became patriotic Hindus when they gave up eating beef and joined in the defence of Assam against the Muslim and the British invasions. Group prayers have a psychological and strengthening influence.

MYTHOLOGY

Religious lore includes mythology, simplified relationships between gods and men, and the creation of the earth and the heavens, etc. The Hindu mythology is very rich since they counted as many gods as men. The Hindus counted time in millions and billions of years. The Hindu view of creation matches almost the modern view of science and reason. The creation and the reabsorption of the physical universe occurs in cycles as if it is the activity of a giant black hole. The Hindu mount Olympus is the region of Kailash-Mansarovar on the border between India and the Tibet region of China. The *Puranas* and the *Vedas* talk of struggle for supremacy between the gods and the *asuras* (demons) and the leaders are named in lineage down to certain human royal families. The myths relate to the nebulous ancient history of the marches of tribes from Africa and Asia to India. The virtues and human vices of the gods and demons are didactic for human conduct. There is mutual borrowing between the myths of the Hindus, the Buddhists and the Jains. The influx of the Greeks into Afghanistan and India was another resource for the development of later day myths and for the development of post-Buddhist Hindu society. The ascendancy of Vishnu had its roots in the Hinduism around the Hindu Kush mountains. The *Vedic* ascendancy prevailed in the river valleys of north-west India while in the east and the south, the Brahmins and the Shiva worship with chief centre at Varanasi were paramount. Brahmins officiated at all worship even in the worship of the forest tribes. All beliefs inter-penetrated, making India a melting pot of religious beliefs allowed freely to interact with each other. The melting pot was enriched further by the admixture of Islam and Christianity in spite of separatist aims of the Muslims. The Islamic mythology is fully borrowed from the Jewish one. Islam overthrew Arab divinities which were mainly borrowed from Hindu-Buddhist lore. Christian mythology echoes the miracles and lore of the Hindus though they have disbelief in the original Hindu-Sikh miracles. Identification of a religion with its authentic mythology is childish since most myths are freely travelling between various religions.

The *Ramayana* and the *Mahabharata*, the two Hindu epics, are full of highly entertaining and ethically instructive material.

CREATION

Each religion has some mythical ideas about the formation of the universe, the earth, first man, etc. Even today the scientific theories are rather vague and speculative. We appreciate the advice of the Buddha against speculations about the nature of God, soul or creation since all such speculations are barren so far as evolution of the society and mankind is concerned. One could hold steadfast to one's own faith but one need not despair about someone else's faith or lack of faith. The myths of genesis without the underpinning of faith are merely childish guesses from observations about birth and death. Sky is often accepted as a canopy studded with stars and the floating earth is made steady by a tortoise etc. etc. and that God needed well-earned rest after completing the creation of the universe. Anything mysterious was the handiwork of a specific god like the gods of fire, wind, or rain. The current scientific theories are not final either. Strangely, the mythical explanations, believed by the Hindus, are pretty close, to modern ideas. *Pralaya* or the end of the universe occurs when God inhales the whole universe and creation occurs when He exhales, all in cycles. The scientists now believe that galaxies vanish into black holes and perhaps when the black hole becomes too large and unstable, it spews forth galaxies in spurts as if a divine player is blowing smoke rings. We now know that satellites *issue forth* through atomic explosions from parent planets, but ancients had an everlasting god responsible for each moon or a ring around a planet. According to scientific thinking, the natural endowment of characteristics of matter and radiation set the newly manifest universe on the path of evolution : galaxies, stars, elements and planets, satellites, nuclear explosions, fields and radiation, molecules and genes, life and decay, red giants, white dwarfs and black holes being the unmanifest state of the universe. The cycles can be unending with each cycle taking few billion years.

The Hindus have surmised the exact age of the universe which is pretty close to the currently accepted age of the earth.

DEITY

God was at first supposed to be the supreme among all gods, each having specific role. The gods were endowed with almost human qualities and failings. They could be influenced by prayer and humility. Later, God came to include whole universe including all the gods. God was regarded as the consciousness, an objective reality pervading the entire universe almost like a quantum mechanical force field which determined the continuing development from past to future. Human reason required some explanation for the non-uniformity of initial conditions of all newly born. The explanation coined was that there is transmigration of souls and there is rebirth after death. The initial conditions of new birth are determined by the contamination of good or bad deeds from earlier lives still clinging to the reborn soul. The faith in after life is heaven or hell is the same sort of thinking in other religions. Hindus combined the two concepts by believing that the soul is reborn after a calculated time spent in heaven or hell so that it can have a fresh chance on the ladder of evolution. The heavens or hells have not been located by the astronomers in space, though the seers during their meditation freely tour in these places and bolster the faith of others. The concepts of after life have proved a good policeman for disciplining people in this life. All religions favour a life of righteousness. The existence of evil is an enigma for the faithful. The Druses believe that God and the devil hold the destiny of man turn by turn. It is established that good and bad are terms related to the values of the society and the aim of minimum damage to others. Man's thinking is complex and his actions often result from undetermined hidden drives. Even his evil deeds deserve rational thinking and forgiveness. A secular person will pursue the dictates of his own conscience. He ought to take full responsibility for his actions and not load God with his own miscalculations.

The theists, when find communion with formless God to be not too easy, replace him with a *sakar* (with a form) god. They regard idols and ikons as communicating channels. Thus developed various forms of *bhakti* or devotion to a caring god. Such gods among the Hindus are Shiva, Rama or Krishna, and Shakti or goddess Durga. The Buddhists worship various Buddhas or Bodhisattvas. The Jains have Arhats and Tirthankaras. The Sikhs and many other brotherhoods find their preceptor or Guru indistinguishable from God. When one worships any deity or holy article sincerely, the mind receives coveted enlightenment. This is an article of faith among the secularists so they find all faiths as based on true experience.

PRAYER

In case of certain humanist systems not adopting a definite creed, prayer takes the form of individual or group meditation. Prayer in general enumerates the virtues of the deity hoping that a fraction rubs off on the person who prays. The Hindu and Sikh prayers specifically ask for the welfare of all. Muslims pray only for the strengthening of the coreligionists. The Christians pray for the spread of Christian solace among the heathens. Group prayers are close to group therapy. From general experience prayer is very useful to an individual and the easy success brings fresh converts to prayer.

PRIESTS AND PRIESTCRAFT

At the start of religion, anyone could carry out prescribed rituals and prescribed ways of worship, but soon certain specialists were trained in the stylised movements and intonations and called to carry out the worship and lead the prayers. Such priests also became adept in reading omens and predictions usually hedged by conditions to ward off any slippage. The credit for some humanity and some refuge for the oppressed goes to priests. They also taught rudiments of book reading and memorising of religious texts to children destined to be priests. Among the Hindus the priestly class of Brahmins came to occupy top position among the populace. They had all the human rights and also chose to follow moral lives. They usually aspired to position of teachers and advisers and never of direct rule except in the eighteenth century when Marathas chose the chief minister who was a Brahmin to be the Peshwa or head of state superior to all the military commanders of the Maratha confederacy.

Muslims do not have a priestly class but they are under the rule of the *Koran* as interpreted by the Ulema or the pedagogues who bolster the orders from the *Koran* by the record of actions and reactions of the prophet. The instruction to follow the footsteps of the prophet is so strong that there is pressure for conformity to the extent of becoming an automatic clone of the prophet. Most modern knowledge can be consigned to the dust-bin so that no one may go forward but stay riveted to the times of the seventh century Arab tribal life. There has not been possible any modern reforms in Muslim society. Most reformers are called un-Islamic and accused of going against the teachings of the *Koran* and the *Hadis* (life and actions of the prophet). The pirs who are influenced by the views of the Iranians, Hindu *yogis* and the Buddhists, spread and believe in the relationship of love with God, are often at loggerheads with the Islamic state usually aiming to remain in the good books of the Ulema, and the entrenched elite. The Buddhists, who have no priests, were the first to organise the religious orders of monks and nuns in the Sangha, which became a model for later day monks and nuns among the Jains, the Christians and the Hindus. The Sikh Gurus were against having priests as intermediaries between the Sikhs and God. Quakers among Christians have no use for the priests. In India Brahmins infiltrated in every sect to take over the tasks of priests. They usurped most of the Sikh gurdwaras as *mahants* and the Sikhs had to wage a struggle under the inspiration from the British to overthrow the *mahants*. The British were aiding the Sikhs to achieve a separate identity from the Hindus and wean them away from the Indian struggle for independence. Even after independence some Sikhs favoured an independent state for the Sikhs. In fact, Hindus and Sikhs were like warp and woof of the Punjab society. In many families the elder brother was baptized as a Sikh while the younger ones were deemed Hindus. The Khalistan slogan was invented by certain Sikhs settled abroad and was aggravated by some *granthis* and *raagis* and attendants of certain gurdwaras who had dreams of supreme power over the Sikh state from the sacred seats of the Sikhs. For a secular Indian, priests cannot be allowed to subvert democracy in their own favour. The priests may be given due recognition in religious matters. In a multireligious country, the humanist approach is necessary.

Guidance of a *guru* is still held in high esteem and is very comfortable for an average person. We have many new sects with own *gurus* e.g. Nirankaris, Ismailis, Radha Soamis, and followers of the late Sai Baba, Swami Chinmayananda, etc. There are scores of living godmen who interpret the scriptures and mainly the Hindu philosophy to their followers. There are similarly many *takya-nishins* or Muslim and Sufi venerables with idolatrous followers among the peasants around their seats of action.

RELIGIOUS OBLIGATIONS

Every religion punctuates human life with certain rituals e.g. at birth, *mundan*, sacred thread ceremony, marriage and rituals connected with death and post-death charities. Strangely, there are no inescapable rituals or rites for becoming a Hindu or for maintaining that status. A dip in the Ganges can remove the ill-effects of any transgression. The sacred thread, that the Hindus or the Parsis elect to wear, is like the *Dharma*, fragile like it and binding like it. Besides the customary rituals, the Muslims have ritual circumcision, and reading of the *fatiha* after burial. In addition, every Muslim is enjoined to go on pilgrimage to *Kaaba*, or the sacred stone at Mecca, in Saudi Arabia, to commemorate the ancient worship in Arabia presumably an offshoot of the ancient Shiva worship.

A secular person himself follows the obligations common in his or her family and allows the free observation of any rituals by others so long as they are not against ethics and morality and do not create hatred of others.

We thus conclude that religion is fairly universal with minor alterations and has been spreading because of its favour with society in general and help in the mental peace of individuals, especially when beset with difficulties. It also adds meaning to life and give everyone some hope when at the brink of exit from this life.

4

Some Milestones in Philosophy

SIX SYSTEMS OF HINDU PHILOSOPHY

Vedas had been composed few centuries earlier and to avoid errors creeping into the sacred texts, the disciples of the Brahmin teachers made them commit the texts to memory. Thus the texts were retained in all purity. Contained in the *Vedas*, besides the magical incantations for worshipping the gods and making sacrifices to them through consigning the sacrifice to the sacred fire, were statements about creation, soul and admission of lack of knowledge of first cause and timelessness of the universe. The *Vedas* preserved also the views of Brihaspati, the arch hedonist and Charuvak the dissenting atheist. There are speculations on all kinds of philosophic issues. This effort resulted in the crystallization of six systems of Hindu philosophy. *Puranas* try to make all the gods relate to the supreme God. The teachers could pay homage to all the *Vedas* but specialise in their own chosen aspect of philosophy. The six systems were : *Purva Mimansa*, *Sankhya*, *Yoga*, *Nyaya*, *Vaiseshaka* and *Vedanta*. These took about a millennium to surface and the Buddha's advent was in the middle of this millennium, so the later systems were post-Buddhist and the composers were well-versed with the arguments of atheists and non-believers. In the Indian phraseology, an atheist is one who does not revere the *Vedas* as the epitome of all knowledge. Disbelievers in God or soul are not called atheist even when they argue against God. *Purva Mimansa* treats the *Vedic* incantations as gods and capable of making good the desires of the worshippers. *Sankhya* is, on the contrary, a rational philosophy making God superfluous. The Buddhist philosophy as well as Jain one lean on

Sankhya principles. *Nyaya*, and *Vaiseshaka* are theist as explained in detail by Vachaspati Misra who produced a voluminous commentary. *Nyaya* purports to give aid to debaters by enunciating the requirements of logic, *Nyaya* system deals with the structure of knowledge. The *Yoga* system deals with unification of soul and God. It is mysticism made accessible to all. *Yogis* believe in working miracles and attainment of miraculous powers. The *Vedas* hint that God is immanent and pervades everywhere. The *Advait Vedantist* find soul of man to be identical with God. The *Vaiseshaka* maintains that the complex world cannot be made by chance and cites this as the proof of belief in a Creator. The *Brahmsutra* (*Vedanta*) regards the universe and the creation as a sport of God. Kumaril (ninth century A.D.), a *mimansak*, attempted to rationalise the magical nature of the *Vedic* texts. Development of Vedic religions led from polytheism to monotheism. Harihara (eighth century) refuted the proof by inference of the existence of God. Gunratna (fifteenth century) wrote a commentary, an almost gospel of the atheists. Gotama (third century AD) excluded God or soul from the list of valid subjects of philosophical discussion. He maintained that God is not an indispensable appendage to human consciousness.

BUDDHA, CONFUCIUS, MO TZE AND MANI

The Buddha and Confucius were contemporary but one roamed in India and the other taught in China. Their philosophies were quite distinct. The Buddha had been a follower of an ascetic who believed in torturing the body by fasts and sundry exercises to awaken the spirit inside. Buddha soon found the method quite barren rather making one more vulnerable to desires and cravings. He, therefore, by force of his healthy meditation wrested the truth from prevailing ignorance that the real enemy was desire if one were to win peace and soul's salvation. For defeating desire one does not have to punish physically the body but to meditate on the uselessness of desire gratification, for reaching *Bodhi* or wisdom. For defeating desire one has to live a life of eight-fold virtue. It is right living following the middle path, neither renunciation nor gratification. The Buddha criticised the prevailing climate of magic and rituals, animal sacrifice and hefty fees for the Brahmin priests. He believed in reason and was against superstition and soothsayings of astrologers. He extricated God from the pursuit of evil by placing all fortune at the door of the actions of people in this or previous births. His was the main drive in the growth of belief in rebirth and of necessity bearing the fruit of past actions in this or previous births. He taught by parables and stories of his own previous births. The Buddhist doctrine, shorn of all influence of God or gods on human destiny, appealed to the Chinese and soon afterwards the Chinese became drawn to Buddhism in large numbers. The Chinese had considerable philosophy centred around nature and humanism. The Buddha's emphasis on every man making his own destiny appealed to all thinking people. The Chinese thinkers would easily mix with the Buddhist monks and exchange ideas about their own Confucius and Lao Tze. The *Mahayana* form of Buddhism mixing worship with meditation arrived in China much later and was welcome as elsewhere.

Mo Tze was the early critic in China of Confucius. He questioned the rationalization of traditions by Confucius and still retaining traditional ceremonials. Confucius did not believe that departed spirits of ancestors have any say in the welfare of people, but he desired retention of ceremonies for the ancestors as a mark of respect for tradition. Mo Tze was a peacemaker. Once an aggressive king was subdued by Mo Tze by demonstrating the tactics of that king against an adversary as futile. Confucius and also Mo Tze believed in the Confucian doctrines of human heartedness and righteousness. They favoured agreement with the superior for smooth working of the bureaucracy. The question of bureaucracy was not so pressing in India with a working system of decentralisation to the village level. All embracing love of Mo Tze has an echo in the teaching of Christ that came few centuries later after the engraving of the code of Hammerabi had first taken place in Asia Minor. Mo Tze's belief in spirits was only in deference to the practice of common people. The Buddha addressed himself to the educated classes and did not make such allowances which came later with the *Mahayana* and the Lamaism. Buddhism did not succumb to any opposition in India but the Buddhists declined in numbers because Hinduism absorbed all the good points of Buddhism and confronted *Mahayana* with their own larger list of gods and goddesses.

Mani (Buddhist among fire worshippers of western Iran) worked out a syncretic philosophy based on Buddhism, fire worship and Christianity. This has had a remarkable success from the Caspian sea board to western China across the borders of Iran, Afghanistan and India. Relics of Buddhist *stupas*, Hindu temples and fire worship have been unearthed all over west Asia. Some ancient formulae for reverence of Mani are to be seen in the Himachal Pradesh in India along with a fire temple. The Buddha and Aristotle both believed that wise people seek not pleasure but freedom from care and pain, strife and boredom. Confucianism has enjoyed all along a preferred status in China. One of the rulers made it incumbent to have it in the syllabus for periodical examinations for the selection of administrators. Confucianism meant human heartedness, subservience to natural laws and the middle path. Neo-Confucianism carried out a synthesis with neo-Taoism and Buddhism to suit the changing times later on. It was under the banner of neo-Confucianism that the Tang dynasty of China could boast of ushering in a golden age there. An offshoot in China of Buddhism was Ch'anism or Zen that found particular acceptance in Japan and now-a-days is expanding its following in Russia and India. Yu Lu has this comment on too much emphasis on meditation : as if by too much grinding and polishing even a brick can be converted to a mirror. Meditation alone cannot be expected to bring one to *Bodhi*. Zen is scientific and based on nature and meditation. In contrast, a parallel Chinese formula is Wu Wei or "no matter, never mind", it favours minimum action and minimum change in mental approach.

TAOISM

The Chinese were more practical minded and their idealists also functioned within practical limits. They had always great regard for tradition. The idealists among the followers of Confucius were led by Mencius (371-289 B.C.) who believed that the intrinsic nature of man was good. He favoured the 'well-field' system of political economy and required the head of state to be a moral leader. He believed in the four beginnings of virtue in all, namely, commiseration, shame, lack of modesty and lack of judgement of right from wrong. The awareness of the faults was ultimately going to lead to virtue. All philosophers believed that ancient teaching consisted of Tao, i.e. naturalness. The Taoist Yang Chu regarded all life as sacred like the Jains (Mahavira 580-500 B.C.) Even a recluse values his own self. Lao Tzu, an important early Taoist, desired regulation to conform to the natural way (of the Tao) and with Te the selfless spiritual power. Broadly, Confucianism dealt with traditions and ceremonies and Taoism considered spiritual questions in conformity with nature. All things respect Tao or intrinsic nature and everyone values Te (the power). For happiness the recipe of Lao Tze, like that of the Buddha, is 'few desires and less proneness to split hair'. They could better banish both desire and knowledge. He would prefer people to stay innocent. Chang Tzu held that 'no government' is best government. Hsun Tzu of the school of literati believed in the achievement of culture by man. Li (rites and ceremonies) and Yi (morality) as laid down in the social order from ancient emperors gives refinement and purification to man's emotions. The Taoists found music as an instrument for moral education. Taoists held ancient emperors who first practised Tao as heroes e.g. King Wen and legendary Yu. No philosopher agreed with law enforcement by force. Legalists among the philosophers were considered mean and vulgar. In the third and fourth century A.D. under the impact of Buddhist monks, Taoism became a religion. Han rule governed less as required by Taoists for natural growth of culture. Legalists were dismissed from government posts. After the collapse of Han rule in 220 A.D. the interest in philosophy flagged for four centuries. Hsiang Kuo gave a theory of self transformation. Change is universal and everpresent. The neo-Taoists showed subtle sensitivity and were sentimentalists. Arts and skills flourished. The middle path of Buddhism is close to philosophical neo-Taoism. Tao is a wide expanse and not a narrow difficult road. One who achieves Tao achieves *Nirvana*. He is one with it. Han Hui and Li Ao (eighth and ninth centuries) equate Tao to Truth. Supreme Tao leads one to quiescence and impartiality, the qualities also of the Buddha.

CHRIST

There had been groping in all previous philosophies about the role of love in the evolution of man's march to freedom from fear and pain. The natural choice for propagation of love is the mother. The mother goddesses were conceived in Hinduism and in Buddhism and they exist in all tribal beliefs. Many individuals have practised the religion of love of the biological mother even when she is gone and is only a memory. The *Puranas* are full of greatness of mother goddesses. They have a widespread cult of the 'Mother' in India from ancient times and made her the consort of Mahadeva or Siva, the supreme lord among the gods and intellectuals. The cult of the Mother has an echo in the widespread cult of Mary, the mother of God. Some philosophers do proclaim love to be the most important for the progress both biologically as well as psychologically in this world. Christ was a real revolutionary. He held that love is very important at all levels. Human beings should love one another as themselves. People have kinship nay an identity with one another. Already there must have been many examples of love for the teacher as in Greece and India and conversely the love of the disciple from the teacher as Krishna's for Arjuna. Christ was the first leader of men to proclaim the very much earthy existence of God and His love for all men whatever their calling and parentage. This teaching of Christ has later been duplicated in many climes and at many places, but the first mighty quantum jump was made by him. The love displayed by Christ and his God and the saints of Christianity has been a beacon light for all minds and religious persuasions. Krishna demonstrated every kind of his love to his admirers. And it has been reciprocated by his devotees and talented poets like Surdas and Meera Bai and many poet saints of South India. Even now the Hare Krishna movement spreads the message of love of God for mankind, the same message that Christ's followers have been giving down the ages. No direct relation has been determined, but Christianity came to India almost when it reached Greece and Egypt. The *bhakti* movement in India, which is practically the Hindu religion today besides respectful nod to *yoga*, is nothing but reciprocal love with god. 'Love thine enemy' to bring about friendship once again is repeated in the message of Mahatma

Gandhi. The mercy form of love had good image from Shakespeare's *Merchant of Venice*. The *Koran* also lauds Allah's mercy, though the Jehadists do not allow anyone to receive Allah's mercy but themselves. We are certain that locking of horns between Israel and the Palestinians will end on the touch of mercy and not touch of revenge. The arming of any warring camp with atom bombs and nuclear rockets is the argument of the Lord for speeding up working of love between nations and peoples. The world conscience is trying to forget Hiroshima because of the earlier much bigger tragedy of the World War. But a fresh Hiroshima, all of a sudden, will never be excused by the rest of the world. Unite or die is the challenge of the atom bomb.

SCIENCE

With the advent of science there is some hope that people will not be overwhelmed by chaos that often seems to be stronger than logical expectation. Science strictly seeks truth. It trusts instrumented observations more than appearances which are known to be often deceptive. Science trusts cause and effect, one before the other for most of the occurrences. Only in the realm of elementary particles, very high energies, the relativistic and quantum effects twist the cause and effect occurrences. Science follows truth as uncovered by new observations. Scientific theories are tentative as Jain philosophy propositions. The moment more trustworthy theory appears, the earlier theories are jettisoned. Science advances by discussion, logic and appeal to fresh experiments and observations. Scientific approach and scientific temper are necessary for progress and solution of even social problems.

The problems of ever-dwindling human biosphere per person and diminishing material resources with increasing pollution can only be attacked by cooperative effort using science and technology and not by occult miracles. The computer revolution now in action can increase information and production many times, and is a sure guarantee of human happiness so far it depends on availability of stores. The world has only to reorganise itself to make available secure minimum income to each family. The medical miracles will add to the health care and confer longevity to population along with fresh ways of healthy recreation and pastimes. Enormous efforts are still necessary to provide computer hardware and software to school children and adults. Science education has still to percolate to all minds so that the cobwebs of ignorance and hatred of others are banished forever. Science is the major agent for cultural enlightenment. Science is termed the greatest of humanities. Scientific approach enjoins peace and coexistence. Scientific search for unity is a reflection of basic human values. From system analysis, science advises progress to 'ultimate' analysis which takes care of the value judgement as well.

There is already plenty of cooperation in the scientific field, in international peace, in combating terrorism and elimination of drug abuse. Such international cooperation brings one world dreams nearer. Some empirical science and technology has existed even in primitive societies since it is human nature to think and use tools, but real scientific development has come from the west apparent from long list of genius that flowered there : Newton, Descartes, Faraday, Maxwell, Einstein and many others. Science knows no barriers and it is fast reaching the villages of the poverty stricken countries as a ready elixir for hope.

YOGA

We have already cursorily discussed yoga as a part of the Hindu philosophy. But yoga deserves much more attention, especially when intelligent machines are around the corner. Imagine the chaos that might be created if the machines get ahead of human beings with *yoga* as these have done in the matter of computations, but one can be sure that the creator of a machine will know how to be safe. After all the giant sized elephants loyally do what the urchin of the elephant driver tells it to do. *Yoga* means definite steps through self control, breath control and mind-body exercises, by which one may develop uncanny powers of mind and if one were to avoid entanglements in these, one could feel like immanent God or in special sense be one with him. Incidentally whatever be the merits of mental powers that *Yoga* brings about it is possibly the best system for maintaining human health of all human organs for at least one hundred years which they surmise the usual life span to be as in the *Bible*. I have had discussions with trustworthy men both Indian and foreign who from own experience could verify many of the claims the *Yogis* make. It is, however, well documented that some claims are far fetched or require special interpreters to bring them closer to reality.

PHILOSOPHY OF SCIENCE

Philosophy has only first to learn from science the tentative nature of all conclusions. There is always room for better thought in the sense of more satisfactory explanation of old and new observations. There is an ever-expanding frontier of knowledge and human thought. In science there are only milestones and no final goal lines. Since science is a search for truth, all scientific efforts must be allowed full play till these become acceptable or untouchable from the touchstone of experience. Science only reaches plateaus of understanding from where fresh ladders reach deeper and higher.

The basic philosophy of science is sometimes flouted by scientific colleagues when for the sake of continuation with familiar ideas, they oppose more sensible theories of colleagues. Galileo's case is famous, but there are innumerable instances of this type. One famous scientist once quipped that advance in science would receive a fillip if the rejected theories in science were given a second hearing. Sometimes whole areas become too difficult to pursue and get stuck for want of some costly effort or deficiency in required mathematics or tools and then work on that line of thought is abandoned by silent consent. Scientific issues always beckon one for further effort, but people soon become traditionalists even in science and wish to defend what is to be ultimately abandoned as junk. Science has a predilection for economy and simplicity, nature, however, is neither simple nor economical. Due to limitations of human life, a scientist wishes to cover as much area by a single theory as he can. He is always engaged in unification at the base of various concepts. His search for ultimate basic constituents (particles) of matter or energy is an example. Cosmology has become a parade ground for bizarre ideas to explain the hidden structure of time, space and creation or dissolution. Computers have given fresh tools to scientists for speeding up their model making and their calculations.

Physics and multidimensional geometry, matrices and higher order partial differential equations have reached esoteric levels. After exhausting the potential of a single dimensionless point in the evolution of matter and space, they now talk of a string of infinite number of points as the base thus introducing complexity at the base of everything. A successful explanation must not just explain things that it set out to do, but also predict new experiments and observations. The firm faith in the uncertainty principle has put a period on all predictive efforts about the future. A scientist truly serves the *Gita* dictum that one is only free to make efforts without any guarantee of getting even an applause that may be due. Scientists cannot rest on their oars since there is continuous competition to explain things as well as discover exceptions so that more enveloping concepts could be arrived at. In the realm of philosophy, the Buddha was a scientist and a thinker who did not begin with preconceived notions and linked every step of his thought with truth. Einstein, the foremost scientist, has been also a great religious thinker. He rejected ad hoc chance as being a tool of God. He supported the conception of immanence of God and a mystic blue-print present in every particle of nature for its evolution till eternity.

Secularism and New *Mahayana* are the scientific basis for further development and progress in India or in the world. The twin concepts stand for multiplicity of religions and economic policies without generating any strife. Almost a billion watts of energy is issuing forth from the centre of the earth, will future technology harness it to human use and not allow it to be visible in earthquakes and tornadoes? Will solar energy stored in the oceans become of service to humanity in the ever-expanding needs ? *Yoga* and philosophic striving has shown that tranquillity and peace is reachable at individual level but these must become a characteristic of human civilisation. Environmental and mental sciences are endeavouring in this direction. Can human nature be genetically altered in the direction of mutual friendly feelings and kinship of all human beings, especially when even elementary family life is degenerating.

Jawaharlal Nehru advocated scientific temper to be the panacea for all ills of society. Christ and Gandhi have stressed love and non-violence. Science welcomes these advices. Prof. Weinberg has offered the values of science as model for values in human affairs. The underlying striving in science is for unity and truth. Science and technology is a growing colossus. Efforts must continue to attract brilliant minds to science.

5

Applied Philosophy

AESTHETICS

Aesthetics is a branch of applied philosophy that deals with the beautiful, the doctrines of taste, art appreciation and moods of depression and elation. Most people are moved by utilitarian value of any article or idea but after any episodic concern like war or rioting, the public attention shifts to the area of aesthetics and the enjoyment of art and beauty. It is certain that after the Nazi holocaust, the common people of Europe had an opportunity to contemplate the arts of peace. There is evident a new devotion to aesthetics in the art and architecture of modern Europe. After centuries of denigration of idolatry, now in free India there is revival of sculpture and sublime works are issuing forth from chisel, potter's wheel, looms and forges. Sense of beauty depends on inherited culture, changes in environment and values and contemporary genius.

Poets have an inborn sense of beauty of scene and phrase. Kalidas describes the beauty of his beloved in great poetry. Aesthetically moved genius can touch a humdrum scene into an effective instrument for moving his public e.g. into a beautiful tapestry in paint or sculpture or a touching sonnet. Modern idea of female beauty is linked to current craze of women for outdoors and sports and they are shown as trim players in a fast moving race that the world has turned into. According to Aristotle, artistic creation springs from a formative impulse and a craving for emotional expression. Art gives stimulus to one or more senses, but without aesthetic appreciation, the stimulus stays disorganised. The aesthetic perception stimulates the mind for total acceptance, indifference or rejection. Often the uninitiated look for familiar excitement which is not a symbol of excellence. Art has to inspire feelings that do not mean rebellion against cherished values. However, aesthetic regard is dependent on feelings and moods leaning on the instinctive hold on one's heart. Contemplation of symmetrical design always gives pleasure. From viewing, some simple rules have emerged that define their merit. Such rules are definitive of aesthetics for paintings or sculpture. Simple rules when fed into a computer can give rise to tolerably good drawings or paintings, but joy giving excellence cannot be contrived mechanically. Beauty would excite a spark in any observer. If pursuit of happiness is the goal then aesthetically fulfilling art is the means.

According to Goethe, architecture is frozen music, and symmetry is rhythm standing still. The standing waves on the surface of the ocean make it seem like a giant canvas demanding attention. Complexity has some structure for the discerning person. In order to please, certain outstanding features could substitute for symmetry. Simplicity is tantamount to stepping towards dissolution, while complexity demands creative input manifold. The worship of beauty in a life of culture can easily replace religion. The essence lies in the perfect image in the mind of the artist and its conveyance to the viewer. Work of art depicts beauty and truth. Coarse vulgarity is repulsive. Art will include the artistry of means and techniques. Art appreciation should be completed after many and repeated viewings. If one starts with certainty, one may end in doubt (Bacon). An artist if not recognised practically ceases to exist. It is important that deserving artists (or scientists) are given due recognition early rather than continually allowed to remain under test and scrutiny. Every person is a realist and realism should not be hidden too much in any delineation. Aesthetic philosophy also recommends the middle path. A simple pattern will look monotonous and a complex one absurd and burdensome. The artist should bear in mind the sensitivity, sensibility and understanding of his public. Reality always has some distortions and faults in the pattern in the background. A minor distortion suitably placed without disturbing the harmony will accentuate interest. Artists prefer to use soothing warm colours. In literature, simplicity of style with brilliant turn of phrase, as in Shakespeare, will appeal. The essence of aesthetic activity is the intuitive conception of perfect beauty by the artist.

Croce (Italy – modern period) added utility to goodness, beauty .and truth in any cultural judgement.

Geometrical shapes (circles, spheres, pillars and domes) have a peculiar aesthetic appeal, particularly if sexual titillation is vaguely suggested without crossing the bar to vulgarity. Everyone has an imaginary view of heaven or hell. They will appreciate what is heavenly and not what is hellish. Simplicity and directness have a sharper appeal than verbosity and loud colours. Use of large words by neo-philosophers have less appeal.

ETHICS

There have been never two views about the need of ethical behaviour of human beings. The ethical behaviour portends stability. In India there is more talk of religion, truth, soul and God but plenty of shortcomings in the ethical behaviour of individuals and organisations which have led to particularly dismal situation demanding immediate corrective action. Law on the statute book is no answer. What is required is performance within law whether spontaneous or enforced. The enforcement by peer pressure or even voice of the neighbourhood jointly raised may bring better results as was attempted under the much maligned cultural revolution in China. Unbridled individualism does not lead to ethical behaviour. The stability enforced by exploiting regimes and money making bureaucrats have lasted at the cost of well-being of the people. Religion as well as state swore by ethics for safeguarding their own security. Public was brain washed and set on the wrong track for salvation of the soul and improvement in after life while being brain washed to love *status quo* and God given place in the divine order of master and salve. Morals have developed for group survival.

Einstein feels that morality and ethical behaviour should not be linked to metaphysics and religion. Ethical values are practical wisdom. Education should strengthen this practical wisdom. It is ethical and moral to be flexible for achieving the goal of human welfare. Our gods were so very flexible for victory over the *danavas* (ungodly). Even Mahatma Gandhi allowed violence for rightful struggle when non-violence would not work. Moral law for progress is non-violence but for protection of society, both violent and non-violent means are moral. Lasting progress is made by the spread of common values. For India, the highest virtue is secularism and suppression of communalism in all our activities. There should be support to merit and cultivation of merit only. Efficiency and loyalty to any commitment, freely entered into, is the highest morality, illustrated in the lives of our heroes both of religion and of state.

The virtuous leader is one who is secular, not trammelled with greed and connections with the underworld. It would be ethical for all of us to carefully cast our votes in favour of leaders who exemplify morality and ethics. A successful democracy has the advantage that it can pick up leaders of choice. Morality, like art, is the achievement of unity in diversity. The right type of man is one who efficiently unites in himself the widest variety, complexity and completeness of life. The root of human behaviour is desire, emotion and knowledge. Wisdom and judgement are the tools to come to a decision. Bacon defines true pleasure as one that gives tranquillity and repose. Urban sensualism and immorality or individualism without conscience and honour when blindly pursued lead to ruin.

EDUCATION

Education is most important so that every generation can add to the sum total of human knowledge. Education is a continuous process and does not end with school. Education of children is particularly important since it is here that values are firmly established and rounded by home life and later by the participation in society. Values cannot be implanted by hypocrites. This is especially to be taken into consideration when confirming school teachers and principals. Teachers should be such as are satisfied with their simple life. Women make better elementary school teachers, particularly if they are (or have been) part of happy families. Women can show forbearance and face difficult situations in their stride. Non-teaching school staff should also be carefully selected so that none has dubious connections and undesirable habits or bluff behaviour with children.

Plato and his circle discussed the topic of education very often. He recorded the observation that it would be best if child's potential and aptitude or intelligence were correctly assessed at start. This will enable the authorities to sort them out and train for specific professions and develop the particular abilities and skills. This has often been attempted but never in a scientific manner except the current efforts to periodically determine their aptitudes and to give them intelligence test batteries, but the study is usually not pursued till the maturity of same subjects. Greek saw the world to be peopled with a majority of slaves and few free men and owners of slaves. The education then was restricted to the moneyed people who were not slaves, or about one-fourth of the population. The girls stayed at home. In Muslim countries almost same holds. The ratio of school-going girls to boys is very low. The three R's and general topics of culture, hygiene, deportment and customs were taught. If a child showed ability to learn classics, he was accepted as a pupil by a senior for specialisation as a philosopher or literary person. The skills usually were learnt at home from father or in a home industry or profession. Only now the psychologists have developed test batteries for determining the intelligence and aptitudes that can guide the child and its parents to a proper professional training of the child. In a free society, this is not always possible. The desires of the child and the family and financial constraints often prevail.

The Indian system was pursuing the same type of education except that they made an effort to sort out children of various leanings from the accident of their birth. Children of Brahmins were considered to be fit for study and teaching, of Kshatriyas for defence forces, the children of Vaishyas for business and industrial skills or farming and marketing. The children of Shudras for engaging in hygiene and cleaning the environment, agriculture and animal husbandry, but asceticism was open to all. This caste system was considered as ordained by divine law and based on past *karma* of the individual souls. This religious underpinning was so solid that various castes continued to live as cogs in the Indian civilisation without any effort to rebel. The rights of various castes were also graded. The Brahmins constituted the ruling class vowed to life of simplicity and morality. This has been the philosophical ideal. With the passage of time India had about the same type of education and education policy as the rest of the world i.e. families governed the child's education and it had limited openings for future. It is only in last few centuries that training has been in large guilds or cooperative village industries and now all skills have dedicated institutions and so the ancient sorting of kids is not tenable and people follow modern trends in education and training with the limited facilities. The country is doing its bit to promote education and deportment of Shudras and poor people by special concessions and professional openings for them. Indian leaders in government and industry now come from all castes, all religions and all levels of society. Special efforts are still needed to educate the poor regarding their rights and openings waiting for them.

The values are implanted in the child partly at home and that is why there is particular effort for the education of the girl child. The playground for children must be made a healthy place where he is welcome and where he loves to go. The parents and elders have to be careful how they themselves behave with others in the presence of children. A child is particularly attentive and critical of any false actions by them. Bickering and hypocritical adults would become easily their role models. Every child should be taught the character and the achievements of world's great men and women, especially those who have contemporary significance for them and can excite them to pursue similar works. They should be taught to align themselves with larger and larger groups reaching the whole world. The ethical and moral values are essential even superseding conventional religion, asceticism, *bhakti* and prayers. Traditions should be imbibed by children without pressure and by evolving choice. Educational incentives are well-known and constitute a welcome spur.

The values of secularism, work culture and equality in rights and duties have to be inculcated both by precept as well as example. Children have to be guided into good reading, healthy entertainment and to be selective when the adults are exposed to all kinds of trash on the electronic media and the screen. They can be easily involved in clean sports and good friends other than continuously being swept away by TV cartoons which are more often senseless and present a caricature of life. India can afford many experiments in educational organisation and technology so long as the national goals of integration, development, discovery and support of genius are kept in sight. According to Bhrigu's code, a youth who habitually reveres the aged, progresses in four things : reputation, knowledge, fame and strength. Traditionally, a child is expected to get up early in the morning and greet their elders and after exercise and routine bath have breakfast before beginning the daily programme of study and play. In ancient *gurukuls*, the student used to live in the *guru's* home. There was close relationship between the teacher and the student and the student learnt and practised all the time. Even now music and dance is learnt in this style. Tagore planned his school in the same style. Even today there is need to provide residential studentship of a longish duration to dedicated students in the homes or in direct responsibility of famous teachers, scientists, engineers etc. In this way, the student spends few hours each week at least in the company of the teacher.

Prof. Feynman as well as Tagore agree that the learning process is best when it is given through natural curiosity, and skill of the teacher to raise questions and give answers. The education has to be such that the child on growing up has the confidence to tackle any problem. He should possess good capability in the subject of his choice, besides working knowledge of the use of computers and other Information Technology (IT) devices. Education as well as science is to understand and solve and not just gather all kinds of detailed information important for going through quizzes and social intercourse but not so much for specialisation. Treading innovative pursuits is important which alone adds to the human knowledge and understanding of complexities of life and the universe. According to the *Vedas*, austerity, self control and meditation are the foundation of knowledge. Earnestness leads to knowledge.

According to Plato, the essence of higher education is the search of some ideas, then their further evolution and development including those of their offshoots and applications. The Chinese system of selecting administrators through scholastic tests has now become standard practice in the world. The democracy of schools is hundred times better than what one selects by ballot. Mahatma

Gandhi as well as John Dewey feel that education must not be just book learning but could be imparted during the practice of a craft. This implies the possibility of school-going kids to be educated while working in neighbourhood industry provided the interests of childhood are not lost to the child. Education could also mould the mind of the student that he begins to admire wisdom more than wealth. Education promotes the vitality of individuals as well as nations. Education can assist one to drive out the hankering for possession. Hindu wisdom dictates : know thyself and avoid excess. Colleges and universities must cooperate and collaborate in providing superior instruction in many new fields. Voltaire regards life and creativity as synonymous. Science teaches the value of rational thought. Uncertainty is a part of scientific culture. Plato listed in the order of importance : wisdom, courage, prudence and justice. Indian goals covered wealth, love, discrimination and *moksha* (salvation of soul).

Metaphysics deals with what lies beyond experience where neither observation nor reason have authority, only intuition and imagination have importance. Rightness of any action is best determined by its consequences. According to Goethe, reason and science are the supreme strength of man.

VALUES

The question of values has been uppermost for most philosophers. In the ultimate analysis, the touchstone on which one decides whether the next step was right or wrong, is values he has cherished. Only such values prevail as promote one's interest along with that of the community. Actions conforming to one's values increase self esteem. Certain values have been regarded as part of human nature e.g. love of truth, forgiveness, hospitality and obligation to meet demands of duty. Trusting one's conscience is also one value. One with true regard for his value, like help to the weak fallen on his mercy, will make any sacrifice to sustain his value as is done by any hero and the whole community of Rajputs in Indian history who would give succour to even a well-known enemy if once he has been given asylum. Values determine worthwhile goals. Sometimes tactics dictate action at variance with cherished values. Even Lord Krishna has used such tactics provided the goal is clearly in consonance with the moral values sought to be sustained. The communist lenience to other political parties in China was a tactic that determined their violent suppression once they were out in the open. Secularism and non-alignment were adopted by many weaker nations during the cold war. Most values have evolved out of humanism and ancient heritage. They change slowly their content and relevance. Values become widely accepted if these promote stability and prosperity e.g. honesty in business deals. In a climate of inefficiency and laxity in supervision, public recognises the advantages of corruption which flourishes in spite of moral repugnance to it. The answer to corruption, besides strengthening the moral values, is thorough investigation of slightest hint of inefficiency and ignorance in the administrative apparatus. For this purpose the investigating agencies have to be strengthened and the media have to pursue a code of ethics framed by them for progress and maintenance of self image of constructive effort. Totally new values are formed depending on changing environment and contemporary needs. At one time, going to colonialist jail was a sign of moral superiority in India. Among the corrupt rich after Independence, an income tax raid became a symbol of riches. Regard for merit, once regarded as an obvious value, became downgraded by misplaced zeal in foisting less capable persons belonging to certain classes in the country. A better way would have been special effort to bring them up to merit standard and not to lower the merit criterion. Individuals known to be selfish and greedy get elected to our policy making bodies because the values for political election are without moral consideration and appeal only to power hungry political cliques.

The whole of *Ramayana* is around Rama's regard for fulfilling one's word once given. Countless sacrifices have been made following this principle by women of India, by the Sikh Gurus and many heroes of fact or legend. Certain people, especially the fanatics of every religion or ism, hold the public hostage over trivial matters. People resort to strikes, *dharnas*, fasts unto death, burning of public property, all of which is just like cutting one's nose to spite oneself. The authorities must erect sensitive ears and noses to identify and nip disaffection at the very start or even remove the offending steps within reason. The Japanese have invented much less harmful ways of protest without impinging on the efficient running of the state or industry. Most Hindus are vegetarian and revere the cow, still slaughter of cattle and mistreatment of animals in general continues though the Jains do look after injured birds and cattle. Humane treatment of all creation is part of our values covering non-violence and vegetarianism. Incentives could be created to spread this value. Values cannot be forced on unwilling souls.

Perhaps we have to learn fast the fast spreading consumer culture and the aimed supremacy of the market place. This trend is likely to make us bankrupt with glittering façade of certain city markets. The international climate of anarchy and state terrorism does not permit us to stretch our resources to keep up with the Joneses regarding armaments, fast communication, etc. Guru Nanak preached and practised simplicity, accepting even hospitality only from simple households. Today virtue is seen only in riches ! We welcome virtuous people to be rich but they could be virtuous who do not happen to be rich and there should be more respect for them. In the recent past, Gandhi was the architect of new value system that won us our freedom. Now we are free to adopt values and policies that have stood us well in the past or are demanded by modern developments, like punctuality, efficiency and honesty in word and deed. The value system in science and technology fits in also with truth and morality, that of patience, hard work and recognising creativity when hinted somehow. Prof. Weinberg has offered values in science as a fit model for values in human affairs. Science nourishes a theory and then jettisons it for a better one. Science does not believe in finality of scientific knowledge. The conclusions are tentative but satisfying with the evidence one can produce.

Social merit will be the chief external criterion of the validity of new values. In the past, work was a negative status symbol. On the other hand, new competitiveness in the world demands a work culture to be embraced particularly by the educated and the rich, others are already familiar with work culture. New value of *kartavya* or duty undertaken must be stressed. Secularism is the cement for welding solid the Indian nation. India has to pull together to have its counsels heeded outside India. Aggressiveness in faith whether

Hindu, Muslim, Sikh or Christian has no place in India of equal rights and open society. The Indian mind has always been Catholic in outlook. The Indian philosophy regards truth and happiness to be the essence of being. They had standard safety valve for debate and victory in debate. The Kumbh Melas provide the Hyde Park type of vast forum for discussion and future growth of vibrant ideas. Swami Dayanand used a Kumbh Mela to disclose his discovery of Aryan ways of ancient India. There was never a conflict with the scientific explanations of natural events and evolution. The Indian astronomers and mathematicians were quite aware of the shape of the earth, the revolution of the earth around the sun or the cause of eclipses, but they allowed the cult of charity to spread, by the populace feeling they were aiding the liberation of the sun or the moon from certain obvious calamity. This added poetry and festivity to Indian life.

Since 1857, the colonialists diligently nourished the weeds of communalism, the harvest we got was of communal voting and finally partition of India. The partition saga has not yet ended and communalists and terrorists are active dismantling hard earned unity in certain states and pockets. The Indian religious leaders must come up with the revolutionary doctrines that liberate their religion from the illiterate priestly classes and obscurantists. The enlightenment of Lal Ded, the Vaishnava saint turned Sufi, needs many St. Peters to illuminate Indian Islam. Militancy of the middle ages will be a throw back for any Indian group or for the whole of India.

Prof. Kurtz (1968) believes that it is a concern for humanity to free moral values from theological dogma, basing them only on present needs and social demands.

Values govern the self image as well as public esteem and the pecking order in the given society. Jains hold to the philosophical ideas as tentative pretty much as scientists regard their theories. Reverence to folk belief is a part of democracy. We need not in a superior way look down on idol worship or obeisance as unthinking or look down upon the prayers at tombs of saints as un-Islamic so long as such practices edify the individual and he gets spiritual consolation and spiritual experience. But we must adopt the modern values of punctuality and fulfilling our given promise whatever happens. This last value is not new and has been stressed in hoary *Ramayana* and it is the absence of this value which is the root of most inefficiency in old civilisations. The west has awakened to this value by modern slavery to the clock and advantages of efficiency. It is part of work culture which many in the newly freed countries have yet to grasp since our values have been coloured by the idle rich presiding over the pecking order. Whatever our religion, *modus vivendi* and national interest require all of us to pull together and tolerate differences if the underlying understanding and unity are there.

Our religious *Yama* and *Niyam* (i.e., self control and daily habits of healthy living) are unexceptionable. Still being over-religious and swearing by religious taboos and prejudices is harmful. We can use scientific approach as the best guide along with tolerance and largeness of heart. Our belief should guide us to progress even in religious thought, a progress that we voluntarily accept. We have had the good fortune to have excellent philosophers and guides during the last hundred years including many godmen, Tagore, Mahatma Gandhi, Subhash Bose, Aurobindo, Nehru, Azad and Vivekananda. There is no dearth of guides if we can choose properly. Everyone has a right to a minimum standard of life and to bring this about Nehru favoured mixed economy that allows us to derive benefit from any type of economic philosophy that is pragmatic under the prevailing circumstances. We need not jump to communism or to socialism, while accepting to heed their recommendations for the uplift of the poor and to stop exploitation of workers. Even trade unions have rather a limited role in a democratic system which determines policies in the entire nation's interest. Certain privileges, especially in the matter of educational fellowships and training opportunities, have to be earmarked for weaker sections including tribals and backward classes. The privileges should better be restricted to educational and training facilities so that such classes can start self help than be dependent on doles and favours. We should remember that the Buddhist revolution and Jain views required people to become vegetarian and not indulge in hunting or eating flesh of animals. This aspect should be taken up in the interest of national health, prevention of cruelty to animals and general principles of fair play.

Modern values of cooperation, scientific approach, equality and fraternity are standing developed nations in good stead and will similarly benefit us. Modern values are more based on pragmatism and far seeing ability than based on holy writ. We must, when in doubt, regard the Parliament as repository of all wisdom and allow it freely to legislate except that if a reformed legislation affects only a section of the Indian population, the Parliament should allow a committee composed of Parliament members from that group to finally draft and recommend the required legislation. Any measures that single out merit and talent should be encouraged and not shot down because it favours only limited number and not all Indians as wrongly held from democratic equality. The society has to take steps to pull up India economically and spiritually and national interest must be held supreme by the democratically elected Parliament.

PHILOSOPHY OF HISTORY

History is one subject which is most liable to be deliberately coloured by the prejudices and partial knowledge of the author. History is never the bald statement of chronology of events as selected by the author who may also ignore the true sequence or even miss a necessary link in the selected sequence of events. The author always follows his understanding of the philosophy of history and the reader has to make allowances for the prejudices and the style of an author. According to Rousseau history is the art of choosing from among many lies, the one that most resembles the truth and only that part of history is of value that may have contemporary significance. Very often the historian has an axe to grind since he must get a nod of approval from his colleagues and contemporary society as well as the text must square with his own cherished beliefs and prejudices.

Hegel in his dissertation on this subject starts with the expectation to see in history the unfoldment of the grand design of God when he planned and created the universe. One can expect to see the philosophy of Candide in the making. The historian cheers God or finds alibis for untoward occurrences. Historically, evil stalks good and often overpowers it, but the cycle seems to repeat itself. One can be certain that the cycle can break only once when either there is the end of civilisation or there is the dawn of self knowledge by humanity and they can have own blueprint of stability and continued peace and progress in unity and reason. Any philosophy built on the omnipotence of a caring God is optimistic, though historically, there is not much ground for optimism regarding the desirable ending of the cyclic movement in history. Human beings are bundle of contradictions and in spite of repeated cautioning by great geniuses and personalities, the random walk like progress of history continues. Hegel gives the pride of place among the tools that shape God's design in history to freedom. As the people grow in freedom, they have a constructive flow of history. The history of Greece in spite of great promise at start had a sharp ebb because the Greek society was part free, part salve. The Romans prospered when they brought Roman justice and citizenship to so many, but floundered on the rock of defiance to their imperial sway. Hegel feels that Germany or Europe has best understood what freedom meant when they opted for reformation and harnessing of free talent of individuals as captains, kings and leaders. The German unity of Church and secular state would be ideal for giving effect to God's purpose. The world history gets now and then a new momentum from the appearance of a genius now here, now there. The genius arises at an appropriate time and place to further the God's design for man. Whether it is as per God's predetermined design or not, civilisation moves forward with the creative inputs of all men, particularly of superior minds among them. This may be regarded as a mystical approach to history. In nature, the start has been from chaos. It is now known that even in the most turbulent chaos there happens a state of orderly motion often of long duration but still subject to random dissolution.

The drive in history is from the individual wishes and desires. When such desires are widespread, we get the realisation of such wishes. This brings forth the value of enlightened democracy and of capitalism of many capitalists. In quest of stability and security, people organise states and supportive religions. The multiplicity of religions could result in competitive pulls and even strife, but it is foolish to regard strife as a natural corollary of multiplicity of religions. Where there is realisation that all religions have the same aim of bringing optimistic self-help to individual followers and when there is a secular respect of all religions, history is bound to reward such a society. A secular regard for piety, religious worship and rituals prescribed and practised by individuals and groups is a historical necessity of further progress. India stands on the threshold of this stage. This is in spite of hundred years of diligent nourishing of separateness and mutual hatred among colonial slaves by the colonial masters. The genius of Gandhi and Netaji has rescued the whole Indian nation. India has been lucky (according to divine design !) in her leaders when even the BJP becomes a champion of national interests and the prime minister, a nominee of the RSS, exerts to win over the Muslims of India to the national mainstream even when he has to make undeserved concessions to Pakistan, the self declared champion of Muslims anywhere in the world while dreaming of a complete conquest of the world with the whipped up enthusiasm among illiterate Muslim public for *jehad*, particularly in Pakistan, Afghanistan and Bosnia now that cauldrons of hate are not boiling in Libya, Saudi Arabia and Iran.

India and Indian happenings have suffered from the myopia and wilful misinterpretation at the hands of western historians. They could easily draw on the abuse which frustrated priests of Islam and Christianity spread about Indian civilisation in justification of their exploitation and self-appointed task of bringing light to the benighted souls of Hindus. When Hindus believe that every human being is Hindu since the most unifying spiritual belief of the Hindus is humanism, the padris insist that Hindus at the base are immersed in ignorance and superstition with no Bible of any kind to guide them. Hindus spontaneously show a grasp of anthropology and religious instruction for the illiterate tribals by showing them respect in their superstitious doings and offering them solid concepts for worship like heroes of west's children these days.

The west's historians have often commented upon the other-worldliness of Indian religions as replicating the Christian strivings at King Arthur's court depicted by Mark Twain. In India there are no dogmas and people are free to discuss and accept what suits their own temperament and development. Even the Buddha and Gandhi did not depend on miracles but relied on plain discussion and practical ethics. The religious insight of the Indians, Chinese and now also the Japanese is rather advanced. They recognise the importance of prayer, worship and meditation, and all the time asking people to identify with one another. India can find fault with western apologists for efforts to spread Christian myths and superstitions, but they have great debt of gratitude for the western scientists and explorers who have unearthed from oblivion many aspects of ancient cultures including Indian. Hegel also regards the Hindus as stay-at-home people not venturing across the seas for adventure and interaction with others. He forgets the Indian colonisation of many countries in Asia and the current Diaspora in the entire world was yet to take place. One has to remind the west that slavery was unknown in Hindu culture. Hindus held everyone including women to have souls that were chips of one God and their destiny was to realise their true nature of kinship rather true identity. Indian expansion in the olden days was never superimposed on others but was result of orderly teaching and export of Indian teachers and experts. It was surprising to me to learn that even now certain Japanese institutions formally invite Hinduized experts from Vietnam to instruct them in ancient religious texts and language.

There are now new channels of communication and the world is indeed become small with television, newspapers and internet. The global culture and peace is now much more of a future certainty. History now will be a record of flowering of world civilisation through persuasion, discussions and non-violence. The seeds of disruption in the form of jehadist mentality and feelings of hatred for non-conformists to one's own beliefs have to be erased. Real constructive history of the world has only now begun with the accretion of more influence to the United Nations and efforts at outlawing disproportionate armaments. Now all events should be assessed for the purposes of peace, establishment of international law and police powers to the United Nations and not against some imaginary blueprint in the archives of God only known to the few faithfuls. Peace is the currency of world development. Superstitions must give way to scientific approach and liberal ideas. History is to become history of great inventions and new ideas (Spencer) that harmonize global peace and unity.

6

Modern State

The tribal society was practically communist. Joint family and extended joint family was its successor. The head of the family had full authority over other members. Elders demanded and obtained respect. Everyone earned according to his ability and opportunity and everyone's needs had equal importance. The education and training in productive skills passed from father to son. With the passing of the time the society became complex. Education and training were available outside the family. People in general chafed under the tutelage of elders. People tried cooperative farming and production and then allowed some patches for private enterprise. It was soon seen that ownership brought the best from the producer. Utopian considerations favoured reversion to communism where all means of production were owned by the society and all production was pooled and then distributed according to needs of individual families. Some small communes under idealist leaders were quite successful but communism practised on mass scale nation-wide became a flop. The direct remedy was the dictatorship of the communist party and of the boss of the party. All dictatorship is a failure since no one gives his best for the entire community if his own interest is regarded as nothing special. Stalinist communist dictatorship and Maoist military-cum-party dictatorship also ended in fiasco. Islamic reactionary, medieval kind of dictatorship of the literati was a complete failure with science and technology at loggerheads with traditional dogma. Funding of businesses also became a problem. Patch work reform would not work so long as they keep their eyes fixed on the immutability of their dogma and treat non-Muslims as second class citizens. After two world wars and elimination of communism and fascism all eyes turned to democracy. A democratic government also had limitations that they were to safeguard human rights of all and try to bring about economic equality. They had inherited many problems of aggressive malcontents from old as well as of limited skills and funds.

A country like India, that began very optimistically and fearlessly on the *laissez faire* path in democracy, was surrounded by deliberately opposing neighbours who seemed to have encouragement from suppliers of weapons and armaments. Since it was the time of cold war, India could do the balancing act by its non-alignment policy also favoured by other weak nations. Own armament industry, naval strength and sound finances became essential. It was thus that they had to embark on mixed economy so that highly capital intensive basic industries and manufacture of armaments could be started. Certain advanced nations, notably the Soviet Union and Germany and later others including USA and Japan, also joined when they were impressed with the Indian resolve, her policies and her growing economy. For internal peace, India follows secularism, for economic strength and for mobilising both private as well as public finances, they practise mixed economy which is practically an extension of their secular policies to economics. Mixed economy in the Indian parlance means capitalism and free enterprise so long as it is not exploiting, along with socialism as long as it is practical. Even the free enterprise would be under supervision of the state so that easy access to markets does not swamp the rest of the economy. India is a firm believer in expanded trade and has managed to meet its financial commitments. India has also experimented with communist state governments in Kerala and West Bengal. The verdict overall is in favour of other states which are prosperous with mixed economy.

There is some confusion regarding dispensation of merit considerations towards the upliftment of downtrodden classes. This will only prolong the disparity in social status since the genuine uplift can come only by sympathetic environment and hard labour on the part of the dispossessed. India is now in the grip of better nation-building values and the youth is hypnotised by the gospel of Vivekananda and the sacrifices and common sense approach of Netaji. Once it has been realised that pragmatism is the natural choice of philosophy, mixed economy assumes greater soundness. Utopian ambitions and socialism require a re-engineering of the human mind beyond what has already taken place when international cooperation and the cooperative movement as well as insurance has progressed by leaps and bounds. Spencer thought that socialism was a corollary of militarism.

As visualised by Plato, an ideal state would be governed by philosopher class as guardians. Mahatma Gandhi refurbished this theory in the shape of "Trusteeship Principle". All individuals placed in authority should act as trustees. But trusteeship had already been exploited to the hilt by governments and banks. Barring few honourable exceptions, most Congress men who were catapulted into high positions acted as grabbers and not trustees. On the other hand, India had the good fortune in earlier millennia of having a ruling class wedded to simple and honest living devoting most of their time to religion and good government. They created a morality of respect to Brahmins and elders, ethical life and acceptance of one's station and duties. There was pretty much absence of any class conflict. The lacuna was that Brahmins became a caste and not an aristocracy of schools. People were assumed to have aptitudes determined by birth. This in few thousand years resulted in the dilution of discipline among the Brahmins and the society could crumble under attack from outside. The Chinese set the style of selecting their rulers through success in selecting examinations. This was adopted by the colonial government in India and has broadly continued after independence. The colonial administration assured themselves that Indians could not reach sensitive high positions excepting when the merit was overwhelming. Now the backward classes have agitated and have been granted special privileges towards selection for all government posts. This is sacrificing merit for the sake of internal peace and with the feeling that merit will have many other avenues than administrative services. Many bright young men and women choose and prefer professional and business careers.

India has solved the problem of doctrinaire theories of economics and government by choice of democracy and guaranteeing basic and political rights of all. The philosophy of secularism and the middle path has led to mixed economy with excellent results. This is really quite pragmatic by choosing the most appropriate system depending on the contemporary scene and availability of finances. At one time there was so much insistence on self-help that any intervention of multinationals or uncontrolled foreign investments were untouchable. With experience and necessity of expansion of infrastructure and rapid development of industries, there has been ample liberalisation. We are giving full scope of market economy except for mild supervision that there is even spread of development and poorer classes derive due benefits of industrialisation. In a large country with almost a billion inhabitants, some inertia is to be expected. The oral or written instructions of the government or the blueprints forwarded in various election manifestos are tardily and many times ignorantly implemented. The red tape has entangled most of the government including the courts and the law enforcement agencies. The inefficiency and callous disregard of inconvenience to the public and on account of sometimes deliberate harassment to public, short cuts of corruption have multiplied. The courts and the legislatures are seized of the problem, and the fable of the rich man with rungs of supervisory staff is being repeated. A genuine change of institutions requires change in man. The educationists and many NGOs are working for this. National progress depends on efficient bureaucracy which is committed to national progress. The psychologists could play an important role in selection and promotions of bureaucracy. There is some call for disabling men of poor character and with connections with the under-world from getting elected to legislatures and everyone is now called to account for the wealth he or she possesses. There has been lately a spate of convictions of eminent people on the charges of corruption or ill-gotten wealth. Reformers have appeared in the country to raise the positive human qualities of human beings.

India has given herself a very well thought-out constitution with built-in balances and corrective outfits. The Constitution is not rigid and can be amended when considered necessary by overwhelming majority of the legislators. Our last resort is optimism and persistent efficient effort. Politicians have to work in the interest of the nation and not just the interests of their clan or kith and kin. India or any country needs internal peace and external security. Development will come if there is adequate occupation for well trained workforce. In a competitive world, it is new ideas and creativity that count. The rulers must have good lines of communication bordering on redundancy, with all classes of the people and consumer forums are worthwhile steps in this direction. Santayana advises that we must strive for a state governed by men of merit and honour. The chosen men must update their learning periodically. It is best to permit them one or two young aspirants as trainee inductees. Violent "reform" is seen to be self-defeating.

The civilisation moves forward through evolution, wisdom and appearance of genius. Genius should be recognised early and nourished like a hot house plant. Appreciation and honour are the best spur. It is these that kept up the stability and prosperity of ancient India.

KINGSHIP

Human beings live in communities and there has to be some order and conventions for a peaceful life. The accepted behaviour norms were handed over from father to son. At an early stage people became accustomed to aggression from "foreigners" and random excesses from nature. For mutual help and for resistance to armed attack, they organised themselves into communes or states. The communes had all adults as members and families or guilds elected assemblies which elected their councils or *karthas* who held all control until the seniors decided to choose a new head or the controllers themselves abdicated. Once the successor was only the son of the office holder, the time became ripe for hereditary kingship. Hereditary kingship was a convenient way to choose a successor. If the prince was well trained to shoulder the kingly duties and the elders were wise enough to keep him on the narrow path of duty, benevolent monarchy seems to have been a popular regime all over the world. The Indian books on governance assume the king to be on the throne with the approval of the populace. The subjects had the right to revolt. The king had no divine right to rule but he had only the socially allotted task of representing the state and to guard it, make it more prosperous and to aim to be a maharaja or an emperor of the surrounding states. The Indian past is full of efforts of many kings to become the emperors of the whole of India and to be recognised as leaders of the entire people even when India may not become a unitary state. Very few succeeded in this endeavour to control major part of India. The kings held open court and governed practically directly with the help of their feudatories, soldiers and servants. The kings took care not to interfere with the traditions, the castes, guilds, professions, priests, etc. and the prosperity and security of the kingdom were for everybody's happiness and fruitful life.

The kings soon had a court, hand picked ministers, hereditary heads of endowments, feudal fiefs and trained reservists to be placed on active duty when desired by the king. The king secured the roads and punished transgressors. They particularly controlled the greed of the royal tax collectors and superintendents of import and export. There was every effort to strengthen the secret services for the welfare of the people and security of royal dues. The training of princes to be successful kings was very much in vogue. Such a system worked fine so long as all followed a single culture of individual righteousness and the kings followed the code for kings. It is such a background that prompted king Porus when defeated at Jhelum by the superior tactics of Alexander, to boldly ask Alexander to treat him as a king ought to be treated. Kingship always suffered from family intrigues and Indian kings from Dashratha to last Nanda ruler, Altamash to Shah Jehan and the Peshwas to Ranjit Singh suffered from this canker. The British happened to be the first to awaken to the problem posed by disputed succession and made in England a popular prime minister who wielded practically all the king's power but was himself totally under the control of the majority in the parliament or the assembly of influence. But the Peshwas of the Marathas could not escape family intrigues which partly led to their rout at the hands of the British. In a democracy, the armed forces were given no obvious political power. India also elected to have British type of democracy and in addition they removed the office of the king replacing it by that of a president elected by the legislatures. The world has experimented with other systems. The family problems liquidated recently the king and his direct family in Nepal. The Japanese emperors now have only symbolic significance and are a rallying point for the nation. King has been extolled above all for the stability and progress of a nation. Slowly, the kings ceased to be such paragons and the modern equality and opportunity for commoners to excel in every art and craft have practically eliminated the need of one on which all the privileges and rights can be heaped throughout his or her life.

Pakistan, which has inherited the same Indian culture as India, besides being besotted with imaginary idealism of a theocratic state, has not been able to emotionally accept democracy and is craving to have a king or substitute i.e. a modern dictator who need not establish his own dynasty. Would not the president General Musharraf elect himself a king if only the violent theocratic factions permit him. Alexander Dumas has subscribed to a heroic version of French history of her kings. He has extolled kingship as the flag of feudalism. King is at the apex of all feudatories from whom they draw all their significance. Dumas advises complete loyalty to the king as the Indian scriptures do for stability of the social system. Even in Indian states ruled by petty kings termed princes, complete loyalty was so visible and heart touching. The Raja or the prince was regarded as divine deputy over the state. Raja's actions could only be discussed in reverence and loving awe. I have noticed a full general of the Indian army practically saluting thin air whenever he happened to refer to the Raja of his petty state who had also along with other princes surrendered all princely prerogatives to the Indian government. The kings in India were trained from childhood to wield all authority in the interest of their subjects. This became later to mean British interests since the British became the source and protection of the British Indian prince's guaranteed rulership and they turned real despots within British over-lordship. Still due to centuries old traditions, the kings attempted to be ultimate courts of justice and benevolent rulers usually succeeding in winning affection of their subjects.

True managers were projected in India only under democracy. Earlier, the talent of common people was useful only when spotted by the king or his officials. In democracy the choice of talent through academic tests or interview assessment was relatively more objective. We have to thank the founding fathers in prescribing built-in safeguards against the highjacking of Indian democracy by dictatorship. Though it is commonly held that in times of emergency and national peril a dictatorial government is more efficient and democracy functions much better in normal times as the decisions have to be arrived at after reaching a consensus which can be time consuming. That must be the reason why many rules are suspended during any crisis. On the other hand, India, a large country still steeped in illiteracy and superstition, corruption in high and low places, is always in crisis and many politicians are getting converted to praising dictatorship and would vote for President of India to have all constitutional powers over the head of the prime minister. They want the dictatorial principle to trickle down to the village *pradhan* (in place of the present democratic panchayat) followed by a climb up to the apex authority of the parliament. In fact, any system can be reduced to shambles. The real need is of each individual to be thoroughly indoctrinated for discrimination between good and evil. All the world's spiritual and worldly education leaders have attempted this for millennia without success so far. There is only some better hope for the future with the advances in educational technology and more awareness of the political leaders.

DICTATORSHIP

A descendant of kings is born to become a king. A dictator usurps the throne if the events so conspire. He hankers after legitimacy and builds his own props in various sections of society, but particularly in the armed forces of the country. More often, he has been projected to the top position from the armed forces. The dictator must dissolve all influential agencies of the country like parliament, judiciary, bureaucracy and so on and place his own henchmen in key positions. This is also carried out in democracies when there is a change in the government. While in other systems the changes are gradual and not jarring, but in a dictatorship changes are sudden and accompanied by violence and uprising where necessary. The dictator has taken pains to already put together a support base in the form of an armed conspiracy or a jingoistic political crowd fed on harangues by the would-be dictator or his chums. The 'leader' has to have convincing oratorial skill and an outstanding ability to attract and influence people. He is able to coin telling slogans and use possible opportunities to subvert authority and openly rebel, ultimately overpowering the legitimate authority by conspiracy and violence. Dictator appears only when there is practically anarchy and the people are reduced to hopelessness in the face of rising corruption and inefficiency and leaders with *karishma* that can demand loyalty of the people, are missing. A dictator survives, if he can harp on the base urges of the people to exploit the weaker sections and the minorities or other groups that have wealth or certain useful arts and skills. A dictator could also raise the bogey of foreign enemies and if people can rally around some hate gospel, it is excellent for the dictator's regime. Most genuinely religious people are friendly disposed to all human beings, but so-called fundamentalists have less love of the righteous but more hate for those who do not agree with them hundred per cent. The fundamentalists are the proper constituency for a would-be dictator. Dictators come to power through violence and have their exit also through violence. Certain dictators are hard pushed by international pressure to re-establish democracy and human rights. A dictator usually promises to do so but the future has to be first loaded in his favour or in favour of his political faction. He has first to muzzle and put on leash his fundamentalists and vociferous campaigners of national hates. Free press and Tehelka type initiatives can help loosen the grip of selfish traitors on the national agencies and financial control.

All countries are under threat of would-be dictators and must guard themselves primarily by functioning in the interest of the common man. The laws must be simple and such as can be followed in good conscience by the masses who in India, for example, are illiterate and mainly depend on local leaders better placed in wealth, education or professional skill than others of the neighbourhood. The politicians are out to create lobbies for all kinds of issues and the lobbies are the centre of all rhetoric. A watch is to be kept on all lobbies that they do not reach such an impasse as to suggest taking law in own hands. Lobbies must be liquidated promptly or guided to merge with legitimate political parties. Certain ideologies, when claiming to follow only pragmatic principles for specific redress of grievances, begin to permit violence against the personalities in opposition. Such ideologies and demagogues sooner or later produce a dictator e.g. Cromwell, Hitler, Stalin or Mao.

Indians have nostalgia for kings and might still cut their problems with their politicians steeped in utter greed and desire for power, by electing a king. They are fed with glowing stories of ancient kings and exceptional emperors that laboured for justice and welfare of the common man. A king can easily make a benevolent dictator and is often credited to be such. Let us consider a hero among kings, Maharaja Ranjit Singh. He created his own empire and welded together diverse military leaders in the Punjab and extended Punjab's sway over large areas in the north and in the west. One cannot forget, however, the immense ego that goes to the head of a successful king. Only individuals with great self-control can step out of their own ego. It is a fact that Maharaja Ranjit Singh, an eminent connoisseur of horses, was attracted by a horse possessed by an Afghan chieftain. The Maharaja demanded its sale or surrender as a gift, to himself. When this was refused, the Maharaja dispatched an armed unit to bring the proud Afghan and his horse captive to Lahore. In this adventure, the Maharaja sacrificed seven thousand horsemen till his desire to possess the horse was satisfied. One recalls the fable of king log and king stork. God save the poor public from king storks. All dictators are king storks. Perhaps the Maharaja wanted to prove to the Afghans that the plains people of the Punjab can equally be ferocious in the pursuit of their goals unlike in the past when after the defeat of Banda Bahadur, more than hundred thousand Sikhs were beheaded by Afghans on sight.

Hereditary kingship offers a good opportunity of proper training of the future king. In a democracy elections are swayed more by money and muscle power. May be, tight qualifications regarding education, common sense, physical fitness and youth should be laid down for entering elections for the first time. On the basis of performance in the elections, certain hopefuls could be selected for special training for ruling certain areas in a future government. Such trained individuals could then be coopted at the time of future elections as nominated members of the legislature and take their chance of nomination by the winning political party to government posts directly or first as under studies. In this manner we may get qualified and trained rulers which the country needs to avoid subversion by anarchy, violence and would-be dictators.

DEMOCRACY

Henry VIII of England was the ultimate among autocratic kings. He did liberate Church of England from the Roman yoke. He also disillusioned the British from the kingship which often became autocratic. Napoleon's politics for starting a new Napoleon dynasty on the French throne after their experience of the Bourbons and the reckoning by the terror of the French revolution broke the back of kingship in Europe. The American war of independence was also waged against the extension of the British king's rule over the American colonies. The Delhi emperors lost to the adventurers of East India Company and there was neither a come-back of the Delhi kingship nor the kings of England could maintain a hold over India. The Japanese emperor lost much of his halo to the American conquerors who installed a military chief for establishing democratic reforms in Japan. Now most of the kings have been shorn of their divine rights and some are in exile. The French slogan of equality, fraternity and liberty is the password in every country. The United Nations to which all countries adhere swear by democracy and kings and dictators are on the way out. Nehru was very much involved in the dissolution of European empires. Nehru was a strong supporter of adult suffrage which is enshrined in the Indian Constitution. Democracies have a constitution and detailed instructions regarding voting and voting rights. The entire population of voting adults elect a parliament and by majority vote a prime minister is elected who chooses his team of ministers for governing the country for a fixed period. For India the fixed period is five years, after which a new parliament is elected and the voters, through the new parliament, can have new set of rulers.

The change of government happens smoothly as per the choice of the people. An opposition to the governing party or coalition exists in the parliament itself ready on gaining strength to rule instead of the then government which has to resign if it loses the majority support in the parliament. Democracies are often criticised for taking unduly long time in arriving at policy decisions. Still the democracies managed to defeat the dictatorships of Germany, Italy and Japan. They may arrive at their decisions only after careful thought and winning tacit agreement of the opposition, but they mobilise the people better. A good government has to look after everyone's legitimate interests. Even single party dictatorships fail to do this. They can only suppress the opposition which reduces the strength behind the national effort. People have to feel being masters of their environment and fate to support the administration for promotion of production as well as welfare measures. Everyone has to be assured his human rights and the society cannot stay divided in terms of favourites and scorned ones. The foolish aim of power residing only with a closed group has always come to grief. The glories of slave owning masters, or of pious upper castes lording over lower castes and outcastes have vanished with the advent of democracy and justice long denied has prevailed. Much more has still to be done to bring about economic equality, besides political equality. Socialism has to be brought about by Gandhian methods and not by those of Stalin or Mao.

Most democracies suffer from widespread corruption. The kingly doctrine of trusted agents reporting on misdemeanours of bureaucracy and of those who deputise for the king in various ways, have to be adopted as advised by Chanakya. The courts must be free of all coercion and that will strengthen democracy. The bureaucrats and the rulers in a democracy have to be committed to moral values, nationalism and world peace. This can be brought about by judicial use of religion, education and other constructive activities For millennia, reformers have been busy trying to improve human standards of goodness. Much more has yet to be done. Human character is a mixture of good and evil, of selfish ambition and altruism, of partiality to kith and kin and to friends. Yogic evenness of temper and feeling of kinship to all human beings is still far away. The rulers must have other guides besides the whip of the party to ferret out facts, find where unrest is brewing as there is weakness in the system. In ancient times, atleast theoretically, the *gurus* and the ascetics fearlessly expressed the wishes of the people. The leaders even now will do well to have direct links with experts of various kinds over and above the governmental advice coloured by the human failings of most bureaucrats who are much more aware of misreporting by colleagues and other jealous officials including the so-called superior officers. Democracy does not mean that the people must tolerate inefficiency when it is so vehemently present as in the Delhi Vidyut Board or the house tax collecting and assessing authorities. Even the definitions of their task are not clear to the bureaucratic heads of various sections. Nation-building will proceed only through education and training and fiscal discipline. The public has to earn, save and invest.

J.P. wanted India to have a revolution, Subhash Chandra Bose showed remarkable insight when he formulated policies for free India. Our leaders can safely learn from these stalwarts. Nehru's secularism and scientific temper is still a necessary learning for all patriots. Democracy must not be taken as a static system. It has the best infrastructure for a continuous revolution. Only the politicians and the bureaucracy, that provide the vehicle for change, have to understand and work for continuous revolution. All the fossilized rules and regulations must go. It is the hard work and savings of the current generation that will help the future generations reap peace and prosperity in the one world of the future. Our enlightened leaders, besides getting plurality of votes, must become competent in recognising new scientific and technical openings for the country's youth to exploit in their own as well as the world's interests. Democracy allows the press, banking, education, health services, mining and exploration to function at the height of efficiency and with short term and long term goals and not just drift along at few per cent loss or gain each year. Planning in a democracy is much more than ad hoc allotment of funds and then bewailing the short-falls both in aims as well as achievements at the end of the plan periods.

NATIONALISM AND INTERNATIONALISM

Nationalism is successful only when it is not beset with conflicts at the sub-national level. There is equality before law of all citizens of the nation. Internationalism desires nations to live in peace and cooperate with each other in constructive ways. Internationalism does not mean aggressive or defensive groupism. It is not internationalism for nations like UK and USA ganging up to belabour Iraq. Treaties that bind different nations in exercises dictated by the balance of power considerations is a negation of internationalism.

Nationalism came as a welcome relief after the aggressions under the religious banner of Islam or of Christianity. True internationalism that is all inclusive is visible only now after the establishment of the United Nations, but it has yet to mature and become uppermost in the counsels of nations. The globalisation of many kinds will usher true internationalism when one will be a world citizen with guaranteed rights everywhere.

A nation lives in a nation-state with distinct individuality in one or more of the following : language, customs, culture, values, music and arts. A nation is free from external constraints for development. It is an admission of failure if a nation wants to have special laws for sub-nations within it or talks in terms of statutory minority and majority. A democratic nation is governed by a political elected majority or a coalition of elected political parties and the nation usually has a constitution. All citizens have equal rights and responsibilities. There is no constitutional disability of any segment of the population. In India at present the governing parties have formed a majority coalition, although there are basic differences in the outlook of these parties for the nation's economic and cultural ethos. They are held together by common interest in defence and national prosperity and the charisma of the national leadership of the BJP and the leader of the opposition who is an ever present danger to the coalition and any elements that vacate the treasury benches may make common cause with the opposition. It is good to have at least two strong parties in a nation so that each can accrete strength to form the government or be a spur to cooperative efficiency from the ruling coalition. Indian common law is yet to be consolidated. There will be bound to be special provisions for accommodating hard and tenacious customs in certain areas or in certain segments of population in the large country which takes pride in unity in its diversity. Minority problems will arise irrespective of the size of a nation. Many nations in the world, both large and small, had had civil wars and became consolidated only after the violent conflicts were exhausted. With the current optimism regarding world production and economic ties, the nations have more hope to meet the aspirations of their populations and remain strong.

Modernization requires internal peace and assurance of peaceful borders. India strongly believes in co-existence of all nations and their readiness to help each other in the time of need. We are fortunate to experience the heart-felt sympathy of the entire community of nations in the disaster experienced by Gujarat in the recent earthquake. The key to modernization is self-help, the skills acquired by the native population and efficient management by the technical and managerial bureaucracy. Progress will be conditioned by the creativity and innovative skills of the people. In the recent past there has been streamlining in the transfer of resources and skills from the advanced countries to developing countries. People are aware of the danger of exploitation of backward states. There are guidelines propagated by the United Nations for the selection and working of multinationals. Third world countries invented the concepts of non-alignment, South-South cooperation, regional development, etc. to offset the danger of domination of the world by rich and powerful countries, assuring all the time cooperation with them through the United Nations. For proper supervision and completion of large-scale projects, open society, decentralisation for roping in the energies of many more affected people is necessary. Talent in every corner of the country has to be discovered, nourished and harnessed for happy national life.

Systems concepts, combined with ultimate analysis for the preservation of cherished values and global peace and progress, will be necessary. As an insurance against all crisis, the differences in language, religion and domicile must be kept low and unstressed. There should be more play on the theme of national unity. Law and order can be decentralised to panchayats and institutional levels in the interest of curbing corruption and institutional level misdemeanours. National police and investigating agencies will be required to be strengthened for curbing activities against the national interest. In India it is undeniable that a real need exists to uplift the lowly scheduled castes and illiterate among other castes and tribes. This must not be attempted at the cost of diluting the merit requirements but by judicial application of proper incentives to the young aspirants from backward classes and areas to accumulate merit by reserved financial and tuition support. Within the country, everyone must be free to settle anywhere and backward developing states should welcome some limited quota of immigrants from other states to make up the depleted strength in their workforce and dearth of required skills, teachers and security forces. Even Canada, Germany and Australia use such enlightened policies for immigration control by a system of selection, incentives and quotas.

If any local practice is regarded as repugnant to national integration and solidarity, it should be thoroughly curbed using, if necessary, new laws. History and philosophy should be rewritten and freed from bias of foreign adventurers and theologians who often support colonial sway over weaker countries or aim to keep them in ignorance as preserves for foreign expertise. Conflicts slow down progress.

Free discussion is the best guarantee of understanding of national policies. Planned progress can harness the resources of ethnic diversity, as well as labour and skills of the illiterate tribals. Education and healthy life must be assured for all children and tribals. It is the exploiting classes that try to keep people ignorant. The short cuts of ethnic clearance and expropriation of property of minorities is the Nazi doctrine who had borrowed the same from Jehadists and such believers in God granted rights of masters over non-conformists as second class citizens.

The symbol of modernization is modern communications and ever-expanding use of machines, electronics and computers. Any protest method that attacks communications and resorts to suspension of work must be replaced by better ways of protesting. The domicile qualification may be allowed for ordinary labour or lowest rung of any service. The reservation in jobs should never be at the cost of efficiency and merit. The promotion posts in government or other institutions must be strictly based on merit and length of service criteria. The merit must be determined by objective criteria and cash awards earned in service and not through degrading humility to superiors. (Confucius desires all employees to be obedient to superiors). Disaffection in jobs is primarily because of deaf superiors and bad departmental instructions improperly communicated.

Internationalism is a natural growth beyond nationalism. There is so much interdependence among nations which is going to increase with better communications, more trade and activities of multinationals. The multinationals held at one time as the agents of exploitation are no longer untouchables for developing countries and the United Nations assure us that they can be fit channels for transfer of resources and funds to the underdeveloped world. For stepping up international understanding, regional groupings of nations are even more useful. Tourism and cultural exchanges will further advance international understanding. People are now aware of the danger of arsenals with anarchical independent nations. All armaments should now be held on behalf of the United Nations. There should be conscious attempt to formulate and live with international law. If necessary, an international policing of nations may have to be attempted so that powerful nations do not bully the weaker ones. The bullies and criminals within a nation do require policing, why not apply internationally the same recipe.

Until the world is convinced of the growing necessity of peace and cooperation, there can also be a scheme of global security.

7

Philosophy for Peace and Globalisation

MODERN RELIGION

Modern religion is pantheism or naturalism practically expressed in the writings of Lessing, Carlyle, Goethe, Emerson, Gandhi or Tagore. Most people, however, will admit belonging to the religion of their parents but in practice they will conform to modern religion. There is, however, social pressure to perform some essential religious observances, especially on marriage, birth or death. The rituals are only mechanically performed but the lessons are not lost. It is modern insight that goads us to avoid controversy in matters of religion or to pursue secularism or humanism. Goal of personal salvation is not favoured in the modern age as simply inefficient expenditure of time and effort.

Rational ethics is preferred compared to religious dictates. One accepts the proposition that creative evolution is moving matter to memory and time to free will. Consciousness is the recall of images and choice of perceptions and it coexists with life. Modern concepts of time, reality and change are well advanced from earlier certainties and arrows of eternity and maximum entropy. There is conservation of values. Moral philosophy has direct bearing on human behaviour. Love and reason are the prime foundations of values.

Fundamental changes are brought about by mass movements and economic forces. The exodus back to India of millions of Hindus from West Asia and later from Pakistan (both East and West) brought in new emphasis on *yoga* and *bhakti*. Practically all Indians consider it a form of worship to chant the name of God at home or in innumerable churches, temples and gurdwaras. A recent phenomenon is widespread affiliation to personal *gurus*. Many *swamis* and godmen have an expanding clientele. Most of the instructions still are towards the salvation of the ever lasting soul and recognising it as a forlorn drop from the ocean that is God. Modern Hindu philosophy is the age-old Vedanta and self-realization through *yoga* or *bhakti*, but there is also an overtone of practical steps to build character with the instruction of the masters since Guru Nanak and Kabir. There is a movement for bringing about true equality not only in rights but also in wherewithal. People have realized that the established religion and ruling clergy have collected lot of dross and superstition and there is always an undercurrent of expectation of miracles in favour of the devout, but religion is still responsible for the inner world of intuition, mystical experience, contentment and a hopeful mood that springs from righteous action and the personal mode of worship.

Hinduism is an ever-evolving religion. The Sanskrit word for religion is *dharma* or human duty and thus Hinduism is an interpretation of humanism. Hindu philosophy always claimed its origin in the *Vedas*, but the *Nastik* offshoots, Buddhism and Jainism, do not accept the *Vedas* as the ultimate authority. Buddhism and Jainism in practice are not distinguishable from the religion of the rest of the Hindus. All praise simplicity and asceticism. Hinduism provides for the social and philosophical evolution of all groups within its fold. Only a few decades ago the worship of Shiva or Shakti was mixed with animal sacrifice and Bachanalian orgies. Now, in general, devotees are content with offering flowers and customary worship as in other temples of Rama or Krishna. Hinduism has been given modern reformed look by a host of philosophers, poets and *Bhaktas*, like Nanak, Kabir, Dayanand, Dev Guru, Radha Swamy, Shri Ramakrishna, Vivekananda, Tagore and Mahatma Gandhi and the interaction with many Christian men of God engaged in public health and education. Among the renowned teachers of Hinduism, one can mention Swami Chinmayananda, J. Krishnamurthy and Aurobindo Ghosh. Aristocracy of merit and vote is back on the pedestal. Prosperity of all Indians, internal peace and strength to defend against any aggressor is the aim also of any religion in India. Participation in religious discourses and devotional music is considered meritorious. Hindus regard myriads of idols as eyes and ears of God who they believe is everywhere. The immanence of God has been recently deduced by Wald in his analysis of the scientific oddities that are so essential for the occurrence of life and its sustenance anywhere. God can be best searched for in one's own heart. This is also what the Sufis maintain and that is partly the reason that Sufism in Islam had and continues to have devotees among the Hindus. Hindus do not question the Sufi style to pray at tombs and for intervention of dead *pirs*. Even the tribal worship of trees and serpents evokes respect of Hindus.

The civilisation moves forward through evolution, wisdom and appearance of genius. Science has had more than a fair share of genius partly because it confers freedom and is not diehard for tradition.

MYSTICISM AND METAPHYSICS

Mysticism is a romantic approach to God-head. Modern mysticism is illustrated by Sufi saints e.g. Lal Ded, born a Vaishnavite Hindu and later she became a Sufi saint and poet. She was the first among many Kashmiri *rishis* (savants) who spread a noble variety of Islam in the valley which sought a mystic approach to God and praised piety wherever seen. The population of Kashmir, given over to magical *tantrism* both in Hindu as well as Buddhist religions, succumbed to the new Muslim faith of love and renunciation and also some visible coercion by the Muslim rulers in succession. Genuine human approach is to conform to contemporary needs and social demands. The reality is only reflected in experience.

With Marcus Aurelius, St. Paul or Spinoza, rationalism merges into mysticism. All *bhakti* cults and dualist worship are mystic in substance. The usual logic about God and man leads to chance or fate. Philosophy provides vision to pierce tradition. Physical theories down at the base are highly esoteric and approaching supernatural thinking. Physics is giving up mechanistic or natural models. Metaphysics, on the other hand, is trying to probe supernatural phenomena by the only instruments available i.e. selected or trained minds. *Yoga* provides repeatable training of the mind. As the science of the mind develops, metaphysics may also become a genuine part of physics. In *Yoga*, the individual is progressively developed for metaphysical insight and achieves paraphysical abilities like seeing far away scenes directly, or dreaming true. Certain minds are naturally prone to metaphysical awareness. There are well-known documented cases. The field is also strewn with charlatans and one has to be judicious in accepting all claims. It is agreed by most that radiation and reception of thought occurs. Supernatural means may ultimately emerge from natural laws governing simultaneous movement of many electrons in the brain. The partial awareness of soul as distinct from body in case of paralysed or partially dead person may just be the result of physico-chemical steps in the disintegration of minds during dying.

Metaphysics will proceed apace if artificial intelligence can be imparted *yoga* training. The drumming of a pot, miraculously writing pens and sticks that lengthen in the beards of thieves are proven to be fake. Certain god-men and *tantrists* claim to perform miracles. Some conscientious performers openly admit that these claims are made only to bolster faith. Our preoccupation is not with admittedly fake happenings but with the exceptional events that have no rational explanation like a *bhakta* by loud hymn singing making an idol dance or a picture frame hanging on the wall vibrate madly. I have seen in a crowd ordinary individuals who earlier or later did not claim such ability, actually walking on glowing ambers just because a *yogi* asked them to do so. Such a transference of supernatural ability is beyond logic. Metaphysics is concerned with the functioning of brain which is the ultimate in science. For further work in metaphysics, a background of many sciences is required e.g., logic, philosophy, computer science, cybernetics, etc. Many countries are studying telepathy, clairvoyance and life after death in a bid to better understand the functioning of the brain.

SECULAR OUTLOOK

Historically, secularism stands for education being free of bias towards any specific religion or philosophy. Secular outlook stands for inter-personal relations being based on best ethics and morals. The morals and ethics come from faith in humanism and logic. Often these are the same as propagated by religions or founders of religions excepting when certain interpretations of religion claim superior hopes just because of the particular religious label or believe in their entitlement to special dispensation for their disregard of rights of non-believers. The Buddhists, Jains or Dev Samajists and most communists, who are convinced of the Marxist logic, are atheists but they believe in the natural order of evolution and materialist imperatives as well as reciprocity and the middle path. The saints and the *bhaktas* want one to look in kinship on all living beings and to alleviate pain of others. The western social philosophers reasoned out a case for morality for the well-being of society.

Aristotle, Plato, Marcus Aurelius, Michael deMontaigne, Ralph Waldo Emerson, John Dewey, Confucius, Karl Marx and M.N. Roy are regarded primarily as social philosophers. They may subscribe too to the theist beliefs of the milieu or the ancient belief in the perfect harmony of nature. Their primary aim is to achieve peace and progress in society in the evolving social environment. Indian moderns beginning from Guru Nanak and including Netaji, Nehru and Gandhi base their actions on faith. Treating others as own-self is the highest wisdom. A basic principle is to honour truth above friends. Secular outlook also requires one to deal with others only on merit in conduct and wisdom, and not on the basis of religious label sported by anyone. Socrates even in the face of certain death was steadfast in obedience to laws adhered to by him among others for good life and for the good of society. Marcus Aurelius, the greatest of Roman emperors, besides being a conqueror and a reformer, was a moralist. He personified the teachings of the stoics. In his meditations jotted down by him during his military campaigns, he declared the brotherhood of man and the very much modern concept of the moral unity of the world. This was also the religious policy of Asoka, Akbar or Nehru. He valued good morals, control over one's temper, modesty and simplicity. *The Sermon on the Mount*, *Thirukural* of Thiruvalluvar, sufis, saints and Jain *munis* give the same guidance for a happy and moral life.

Dewey, the American social philosopher declares that morals are closest to human nature. According to him the subject of morals is entirely empirical and neither theological nor metaphysical.

Indian *darshaniks* invariably rope in God and soul, since that alone underwrites their firm belief in the kinship of all living beings. Moral science is based on physical, biological and historic factors placed in the human context to guide the activities of man. A responsible society matches its rewards and admiration to those who adhere to moral action and social responsibilities. The standard of morals is low only because the experience of society interaction is defective. Preaching of unassuming simplicity and contentment will not avail when community admiration is for one who "succeeds" and becomes conspicuous one way or the other. Human conduct is also governed by customs, personal convenience and personal likes and dislikes. It is important to study and develop the science of human nature. According to Confucius, moral law is the fulfilment of the laws of human nature. The life of the vulgar is in contradiction to the universal moral order. When a man follows conscientiousness and the principle of reciprocity, he is not far from moral law. True filial piety consists in successfully carrying out the work of forefathers and transmitting the achievements to posterity.

The life of the moral man is plain but attractive, simple, graceful and methodical. Atheists like Charuvaka or Marx are believers of sense knowledge and believe in social necessity. *Rishis* were devoted to reason and inspiration. According to them, God in his immanence was the source of all knowledge. Religion, however, in the hands of ambitious men became a tool for cruelty and iniquity. Reformers hark back to the humanist roots of society and reconfirm secular outlook over and above religious commitments. People feel revulsion from fanaticism when they observe the atrocities ascribed to them.

One with a secular outlook is devoted to human welfare and is pledged to human rights. He is aware that his personal physical and mental well-being prospers through religion and the able performance of his religious obligations. He gives the same freedom to followers of all religions. His interfaith obligations are centred on humanism and sense of natural justice and fair play. The Buddha and Christ were positive that ritual sacrifices were pointless for human salvation. The Aryan worship was pretty much an oft repeated resolve to win self improvement. The first recorded revolt against ritualism was by Jesus Christ and later by Al Haj, the Iranian

Sufi martyr. Practical opposition to ritual worship was expressed by the Indian saints like Nanak, Nizam-ud-din Aulia, Kabir and Mirabai. At about the time Guru Nanak was singing his message of love and devotion in the Punjab, the humanist message was boldly and courageously spread by George Fox in England.

Indians in general are convinced that the *Gita* and the *Advaita* philosophy are the gospel of secularism when they project the same summit of all worship and devotion. One with a secular outlook will disregard any ancient traditions, customs, etc. that have managed to survive but are against humanism and natural justice. A uniform civil code for all will emerge only when certain groups shed special caste privileges and shun special favours not earned by merit. In Turkey, which saw open rebellion against the Caliph of the believers, now strangely, there is ridicule of secularists among their brethren as American Muslims. Since disregarding the fundamentalists' notion of exclusive inheritance in heaven and special rights, especially over non-Muslims or the waging of *jehad*, the secularists believe in equal rights of all. We pray for success of reforms in Muslim thought and spread of ideas of Taslima and other enlightened Muslims or of Muslim *rishis* of Kashmir.

Propagation of secular outlook will proceed hand in hand with the spread of scientific approach. Both are relevant to human progress. New symbols of cultural integration will evolve. A futuristic solution would be to attach secular prayer places to all temples whether these are flourishing in the possession of a particular clergy or are disputed. Secular prayer places within the cherished monuments and protected heritage areas like the Shinto shrines in Japan will spread the secular outlook so necessary for a multi-religious state.

The education in ethics and morals should be compulsory in elementary schools with illustrations chosen from the cultural history of various communities. The priests of any caste or creed should be well conversant with the rituals of at least one other creed besides their own, so that in poor villages one set of priests may suffice for all inhabitants. The worship of idols, tombs, trees and snakes have all a respected place in a secular country. Any disparagement publicly extended to any sacred object or symbol will have to be treated as an offence against the state. A pilgrimage section in the department of culture could guide inter-religious groups for pilgrimages. All religions constitute pillars of a multi-religious society under a secular roof. Confidence building will require more officers and men to be placed in police and legal profession from among the weaker sections of the society including women. Inheritance laws could be modified so that means of production like factories and mines, or the cultural tools like the temples and schools do not become the private property of incompetent owners. Man is reaching out from the material sphere to that of the mind. He is going to evolve through further capabilities of the mind. Secular outlook is very important for the cultivation of our minds. The global culture will be around secularism and loving care for all mankind.

WORLD AS ONE FAMILY (GLOBALISATION)

The Indian ideal governing its foreign policy is that the whole world is a single family. India's foreign policy can be expressed as a foreign policy of peace and coexistence. Whole world now wakes up to assist any people anywhere subject to a natural or a man-made disaster as in earthquakes or genocides. The world is now taking note of terrorism supporting states and is likely to take measures to eradicate it in its all incarnations. With the world trying to pile up international law and taking steps to get it obeyed by all nations, there is no need even for the existence of international state system when there grows an inter-dependent world economy with advantages of scale in production and some stability in price. Global culture will consist of tolerance, secularism and democracy as first envisaged by the Buddha.

Medical facilities and preventive medicine will now expand to become readily available to all at reasonable prices. Cheaper systems of medicine viz., Indian Ayurveda and homeopathy is now given equal status to western medicine in many countries. There is integrated medicine for the unwell i.e., adopt all or any system of medicine that is applicable and brings about early permanent relief. We envisage tremendous advances in the availability of cheap power from the sun, the earth or oceans or by controlled fusion, and world will be so enriched that all old people everywhere can be granted pension and allowed to indulge in nation building at their own pace. Old ladies at all levels of society deserve a pension since they have spent their whole life in service either professionally or in support of their families. Leisure will be enlarged also for the working population and means found that it is spent in joy and with tangible or intangible benefit. There should be abundance to satisfy all. People could attend international expositions, fairs and festivals. Extended attendance and participation in health or meditation camps, pilgrimages or sports like mountaineering, sailing, etc. will be organised for interested persons who have the leisure and can bear the cost by own money or grants from various bodies if they are selected for such enjoyment. Even the partial socialism of the Soviet Union could achieve some of this. The practice of sustainable development and willing curbs on excessive growth of population will remove major cause of misery and aggression. If the nations get to believe in co-existence, U.N. can be strengthened to look after the security of all and take on the necessary task of formulating international law and enforcing it with the assistance of other nations of the region concerned. Scientific advancement can push back the limits of the human biosphere as well as push forward the length of one's life for success in his or her chosen long range activity.

In the global village of tomorrow, environment will receive appropriate attention. Smokeless fuel, electrical propulsion of vehicles, simple robots removing drudgery from human backs will also usher in universal well-being and pursuit of happiness will be both possible and assured of success. In the present state of almost universal want, economic policy will have to be sighted on remunerative work for every one and an apparent slow march to the utopia is therefore understandable. The children who have to augment family income will be given all help to have leisure for play and education. Their childhood labour will earn them credits when they have part-time schooling. India favours institutionalising of export of labour. So that they work abroad in security and fixed tenure with assured return to their homeland to enjoy their savings from hard work overseas. With knowledge and sciences galloping forward, man is on the road to become superman. Everyone should cooperate that the limited resources of air, water and land last to maximum limit and are speedily increased through scientific research and better management. The nations can master the terrorism threat by joint action and denying sanctuaries to drug peddlers and terrorists.

True globalisation will come only when there is a world government or a world federation under UN sovereignty. The present measures to expand markets for full scope to market economy may not be in the interest of the poor majority or the developing countries, particularly when arbitrary controls can be imposed on exports from relatively poor countries for their shortcomings in workers' welfare measures or education of children and economic aid to women. All this will depend on the greater saleable production in poor countries. Family businesses and production efforts in developing countries should be treated as educative and promoter of technical and managerial training to children who would otherwise become completely neglected and unfit to earn their livelihood. The solution is in more earning capacity of the family which includes the earning ability of children who incidentally also learn art and crafts. Beyond the world government is the utopia of world becoming one family.

PURSUIT OF HAPPINESS AND PARADIGM OF NEW *MAHAYANA*

Global culture will rest on humanism, secularism and scientific approach. Bold measures will establish democracy and international law. Once the threat of war is removed, people will have free scope to develop their living standards and intellectual equipment. There will be more leisure for interesting activities and active entertainment like sports, music and arts. Good food and pleasant as well as protective clothing will become universal. Happiness to the extent it depends on externals will be there for everyone.

There is considerable pleasure in participation in community festivals and travelling at leisure. During my stay as head of a naval research laboratory in Cochin in south India, I enjoyed rich cultural events of that region like Onam, the new year festival of Kerala. One can be elated by viewing at Thevera, the famous gathering of elephant mounted gods and goddesses come to pay homage at the

Shiva temple. The Kerala boat race passed close to our quarters on the naval base on the Wellington island. From Cochin I could also visit Sri Lanka, Minicoy, Laccadives and the Maldives in the Indian Ocean. Maldives is the favourite holiday haunt of Europeans and has good cuisine along with coral reef view for snorkel divers. During the International Geophysical Year, on an invitation from the Scripps Institution of Oceanography, I joined their expedition to Easter Island. I flew down from Delhi to Lima via New York to join the oceanographic ship there. During a night watch, I discovered a sea mount not yet on the charts with us. The Easter Island is an isolated outpost of civilisation, the nearest coastline being a thousand miles away. It is now believed that some fugitives on rafts must have drifted to it from the west coast of South America. I was amazed with my colleagues at the quaint practices of the islanders and the great industry they had displayed in the erection of giant statues of a forgotten leader at many spots in the island. During my return journey I had one day at Bangkok and saw the ancient palaces and temples there. I was surprised to see young ladies worshipping the Shiva symbol at the gate of the old palace. I was told that the worship was for the grant of more off spring.

Happiness comes from many things, firstly from satisfaction in one's job or profession, from congenial family and from good friends. Mundane pleasures come from food and drink, entertainment, sex, clothing and sight-seeing, etc. Some people complain that they are bored one way or the other. Solution for boredom only comes from within. Many claim that true happiness lies in spiritual experience of a lofty kind. The Indian *yoga* gives easy outline for the progress in spiritual sense. One way is to accidentally or by effort meet a person who is advanced in this. This happened to Swami Vivekananda when he was noticed by Sri Ramakrishna, the modern embodiment of secular striving for God through various religious gateways. From then on Vivekananda was transformed and became in his own right a great philosopher and exponent of Hindu way of life. *Yoga* points out definite milestones in the spiritual progress for anyone travelling on this path. One can, for example, believe in his new ability to see into future or at inaccessible places by *yogic* concentration or imagine certain glimpses of past lives or experience conversation with chosen god or *guru*. The efforts involved and the discipline to be followed are quite rigorous and most individuals bail themselves out of this effort and difficult path by remembering the *yogic* instruction not to get involved in such skills and *siddhis*, but to always keep in view the highest goal of moulding one's life to always live in communion with the ultimate reality.

Apart from the theistic meditation and *yoga*, *vedic* lore also enumerates materialism and atheistic doctrines which are not alien to Hinduism. Secularism or humanism and "New *Mahayana*" are all inclusive.

The traditional view of heterosexual love is that the bond of husband and wife is for keeps. Behind the arranged Indian marriages, there is the ideological underpinning of fidelity in wedlock. Premarital sex is against the traditional values. On account of relatively late marriages, people being practical, the stress on female virginity or male celibacy before marriage is reduced, but is reappearing because of the fear of aids and the galloping population of the world. Once discussing the choice of suitable girl for marriage, while I, a bachelor, was keen for a pretty face and educated and cultured girl, Prof. Feynman, a widower at that time, vigorously corrected me saying that devotion and kindness are the most desirable qualities which in the west could be discovered by courtship alone.

In the Punjab, there is a custom that the bridegroom is invariably accompanied by a *sarvala* (literally best man) when he comes in the wedding procession to the bride's place. Whatever the origin of this custom rising in the unsettled and precarious old times, these days it is customary that the *sarvala* is a child between three and ten years old. Hindus and Muslims all followed this custom in the Punjab. When about four years old I was picked up as *sarvala* when the neighbour, a Muslim lad, was to be married and I rode behind the bridegroom on the mare in the procession to the bride's house. I remember my senior teasing me later that I was not contributing anything to the well-being of the bride whom I helped him bring home. Guru Nanak felt that a family man will be more successful in reaching godliness. There is through the movement sponsored by the Moons a new emphasis in Christianity on family life. The wife is the anchor around which the family flourishes.

There are so many scenic rail or road journeys in the world, some of which I had the good fortune to traverse e.g. the rail car journey from Kalka to Simla, from Siliguri to Darjeeling, from Mysore to Oota-Comund, from the plains to the isolated height of Abbotabad (now in Pakistan), the popular destination of Kodaikanal on the eastern Ghats and the journey to Machu Pichu in Peru. Short voyages for sight seeing in the New York harbour or from Vancouver to Victoria or the boat ride to view the mangroves at Calicut are to be counted in the same category. Of course, there are world famous sights of the Niagra Falls and the Grand canyon in the United States, the Taj Mahal and the Dilwara temples in India or the Pyramids in Egypt, or the Swiss Alps. The scenes and views are innumerable and in our limited lives one can derive immense pleasure from such visits.

It is not easy to choose the best scene of nature that I might have seen, but my best bet is on the view from an aircraft over the gleaming peaks of the Himalayas if there happens to be morning sun shining on them. The view of peaks and canyons from the aircraft going to Delhi from Moscow will captivate any one. Among European cities all the capital cities have much to offer. Given a choice, I would take them in the order. Rome, London, Paris, Vienna and pretty Swiss cities in Europe.

For entertainment, shopping paradise and variety in food and fruit, Delhi vies for the crown with Singapore. In Delhi highly cultured dances and music are to be enjoyed for free if one takes the trouble to reach the site of the programme. There are innumerable flower shows, trade fairs and cottage industries emporia. Delhi being an old capital city has scores of monuments and ancient and modern structures for all tastes. Among the cities steeped in legends and history, only London and Vienna equal Delhi. Among the cities of commerce and future trade, Hong Kong and Tokyo can vie with London and New York. For casinos, most summer resorts are equipped. Kathmandu boasts of a flourishing casino in the east, but the variety and stakes are much larger in Las Vegas of the United States.

New *Mahayana* is the pragmatic paradigm of the post-industrial post-unipolar world. Just as *Mahayana* form of Buddhism was made welcome in all countries where the Buddha's message of right action and the middle path was augmented by assurance of caring pantheon with gods and *Bodhisatvas* to whom one could choose to pray. Any possible conflict between various religions was eliminated. The New *Mahayana* seeks to eliminate strife due to differences in religious thought as well as in political philosophies and organisations. External security is most essential for the progress of civilisation. We know tragedies that befell the ancient Rome, the Arab empire, the Christendom, the Hindu India or the Mayas and the Incas. After considerable progress and expansion, these mighty spreads collapsed under barbaric attacks from jealous outsiders. More recently, the British and the French empires collapsed under the hammer blows from the axis powers and the ideological empire of the communists lost its moorings under the challenge of competition from America and the free market. Most of the settled world is now afraid of fundamentalist revival underscored by spread of terrorism, criminal wealth and clandestine supply of sophisticated weapons. Much of this can be countered by a universal agreement in favour of rule of law and by developing international organs of policing. The ideologues' contribution is the framework of the U.N. and the Security Council and the new sanctity being endowed to human rights. Humanism and secularism will break the back of fundamentalism. Human rights will automatically receive the due respect under New *Mahayana*.

In religion and in politics, the New *Mahayana* is the way of coexistence and non-violence. Good-bye to fundamentalism does not mean that there must be a lid on religious development and reform. All reform action will be through non-violence and persuasion. The alternative is destruction through violent wars. Such destruction will be total when push button skill might unleash atomic weapons on the target lands. Even non-targeted lands will be destroyed by such weapons of mass destruction followed by spread of plagues and pestilence. Even countries with large area or population will not escape. The ideal of peace must now become practical peace and cooperation. Acceptance of all mankind as belonging to a single family is no longer based only on theistic belief in one universal God, but on the logic of survival. Pax Romana and Pax Brittania based on the armed mights of Rome or Great Britain did not last beyond few centuries. Ashoka sent out missionaries in peace for right action and middle path. This peace and peaceful intercourse between peoples lasted a millennium and a half. The New *Mahayana* through acceptance of its ideals by the U.N. is for all time or eternity. Socialism and social justice must win over theism and religion by offering it coexistence within the confines of human benefit and longevity of civilisation. Gandhi's spirituality, Nehru's socialism and Azad's interpretation of Islam gave meaning to Indian secularism and mixed economy.

India has been blessed with a basic philosophy most appropriate for world culture and world unity in diversity. Guru Govind Singh has taught that cooperative thinking of plural minds is the wisdom of God. Exclusivism and fanaticism are not specific to any particular religion. Tenaciously held non-religious beliefs can also lead to fanaticism. Jacobins and Stalinists illustrate this, the same was true of McCarthyism. Demagogues and mad priests can goad mob violence. Toleration and coexistence are essential for world unity. In the times of the Buddhist *Mahayana*, India was the Mecca of the civilised world. In the Indian practice of new economy, none may be belittled to show honour to God or man. Neither market nor socialist controls would be made a fetish at the cost of happiness of man. New *Mahayana* assumes the complexity of mind and various beliefs coexisting at different levels. It is against dictatorship of any kind, of wealth or *ulema*, or clergy or demagogues. Any private assurance of completeness of knowledge with no room for progress is unthinkable. In the multipolar world of tomorrow, New *Mahayana* will be the pragmatic paradigm.

New *Mahayana* is the philosophy of acceptance and coexistence. The abstract teaching of the Buddha placing the entire responsibility on an individual for own salvation became the anchor of many peoples of the world only when they became, after Nagarjuna, the followers of the *Mahayana* form of Buddhism that included faith and worship and many godly helpers on the path to *nirvana*. The acceptance of the spiritual experience of every kind is very much needed now. The alternative to peaceful co-existence is only destruction through violence. The new ethics has also to come to terms with the limited resources of the earth and the absence of any direct interference in human affairs by supernatural beings. The scientific miracles will certainly bring about full utilization of natural resources and all have to accept that everyone is entitled to sustenance from this planet. It is not necessary to be a theist to arrive at the oneness of all creation. New values of multi-religious beliefs and pragmatic non-violent political and economic thought will constitute the new *Mahayana* of the post-industrial multipolar world.

It is interesting that the philosophy began with the human being as the focus and it was frankly atheist and humanist. Observe ancient Jainism flourishing till today or the *Sanatan Dharma*. The central Hindu view of true religion is to possess the essential quality of being a human being or in other words to grasp humanism. Soon, however, people had the feeling of insufficiency without the charted ways to appease the gods and the forces beyond human ken. Certain events and upheavals could be understood only by ascribing them to the deity or destiny. Thus grew theism, faith and worship in the prehistoric times. Instigated by priestcraft, the differences in us and them led to strife and struggle. Humanism and the New *Mahayana* are most appropriate for world culture and for unity in diversity. We hold with Guru Govind Singh, the founder of the Sikh brotherhood, that the cooperative plural mind voices the wisdom of God. Fanaticism can raise its ugly head in any system of belief when tenaciously held bereft of humanism and a sense of natural equity and justice. Jacobite and Stalinist terror are examples of non-religious fanaticism. Same can be said of McCarthyism and saffron campaigns. The exclusiveness and the belief that all that is worth consideration is already known to a particular *Bible* or a prophet is childish. Once when I was starting on a fishing outing, I was assured by a child that no fish were to be caught that day since he and his daddy had caught all the fish a day before !

Science and technology have led to freedom and equality. The eradication of abhorring labour and back-breaking effort has begun only with the vacuum cleaning, flush system, wheel barrow and the mechanical or electrical contrivances. A poison has been invented in the form of the atomic bomb. There is need for accepting the nectar and rejecting the poison or to control the application of science and technology. A world at peace alone can banish armaments of mass destruction. The New *Mahayana* as universal policy can assure security of nations' and safety of all human beings. This will usher in the twenty-first century of peace and the creation of enforceable international law established by the consensus of all nations. The progressing globalization of the economy of most nations is a step towards a vibrant United Nations.

There can be no coercion in human beliefs and cherished values. These have to be changed for the better only through reason and interest of the society. A human being has to be accepted as a complex identity which is averse to be circumscribed by limits. The mind can simultaneously harbour different views and do justice to them at every opportunity. The ethical values and human rights will have prime importance. In spiritual matters, New *Mahayana* will encompass pluralism and secularism i.e., the beliefs that direct human beings to resolve conflicts in peace. Poor or incompetent management might cause bottlenecks, but technical progress will eliminate tensions.

The faiths of the *quakers*, *bahais* and *yogic* discipline in human beings are precursors of enlightened life all around. The theists have a conjecture that God is an objective Reality. But all ideas are in human mind and, therefore, subjective. All mature cultures uphold the family and the sanctity of marriage. Prudery in matters of sex was never a Hindu trait. Sex education is carved in stone in temples constructed in the middle ages. Promiscuity has afflicted civilisations only in times of excessive wealth or excessive misery when ethics and morality were being neglected, the trendy mixing of sexes was overlooked. The global culture will find a middle ground around the family structure and limited indulgence in sex particularly in the environment of overpopulation and limited resources. The global culture of democracy and respect of human rights is going to take root. No one may be belittled to show honour to God or man. Righteous pragmatism would be the paradigm of the new culture. New symbols of cultural integration will be invented. A person has many levels of thinking and he can harbour feelings of adoration and acceptance of many different concepts for the elevation of mankind. The *Mahayana* and the *Gita* brought about the acceptance of all religious striving as well as the coexistence of all the gods. The new philosophy is against dictatorship of every kind: of labour, of capital, of clergy, or of demagogues or *ulemas*. Democracy and freedom exist together.

Secularism and humanism can be strengthened by the reorientation in the training of the priests and teachers. For any plural society, any stamp of uniformity or private assurance of totality of knowledge or of guidance is unthinkable. There should be more cultivation of secular virtues like efficiency, creativity and consistency between word and deed. The New *Mahayana* is the pragmatic paradigm of the post-industrial and post-unipolar world. The New *Mahayana* seeks to eliminate strife not only between different religions and philosophies but also between different political and economic policies.

It is the way of peaceful coexistence and cooperative freedom in mutual interest. Gandhi and Nehru have given meaning to Indian secularism and mixed economy, which in substance give effect to New *Mahayana*. Neither the market nor socialist controls can be made a fetish at the cost of human happiness.

Bibliography

Ali Engineer, A. (1988). Sufism and Communal Harmony, *Mainstream*, July 2, pp 19-23.

Ayn, Rand, (1961). *For the New Intellectuals*, New American Library, New York.

Banerjee, Akshay Kumar, *Philosophy of Gorakhnath*, Bharatiya Vidya Bhavan, Mumbai.

Banerji, Suresh Chander (1993). *Society in Ancient India*, DK Printworld (P), New Delhi.

Bdood, Kazi Abdul (1991). *Dildar's Couplets*, Khuda Bakhsh Library, Patna.

Durant, Will (1926). *Story of Philosophy*, Simon and Schuster, New York.

Durant, Will (1954). *The Oriental Heritage*, Simon and Schuster, New York.

Egner, Robert E. (1958). *Bertrand Russell's Best*, Allen and Unwin, London.

Feynman, R.P. (1975). *The Pleasure of Finding Things Out.*

Gorney, Radric (1972). *The Human Agenda*, Simon and Schuster, Los Angeles.

Gupta, M.N. *Gospel of Sri Ramakrishna*, Out of print.

Hegel, G.W.F. (1944). *Philosophy of History*, Willey Book Co., New York.

Krishnamurthi, J. (1989). *Happy he who has Nothing*, Krishnamurthi Foundation, Varanasi.

Moon, Sun Myung (1992). *Science and Absolute Values*, ICF Press, New York.

Mukerji, Vishwanath (1996). *Bharat Ke Mahan Yogi*, Anurag Pub., Varanasi.

Nanda, J.N. (1986). *Science and Technology in India's Transformation*, Concept Publishing Co., New Delhi.

Nanda, J.N. (1991). *Conflicts and Co-existence*, Concept Publishing Co., New Delhi.

Nanda, J.N. (1992). *Autobiography and New Mahayana*, Secular Life Society, Delhi.

Ojha, Sri Krishen (1982). *History of Ancient Indian Thought*, Research, Delhi.

Padmanabhan, Chennai (1981). *Andal's Tiruppavai*, R.P. Publications, Chennai.

Pani, Jiwan, (1990). *Essays on Art and Aesthetics*, Centre for Indian Classical Dance, New Delhi.

Parg, Lowenhud, (1987). *The Open Society*, PWPA, Paragon House, New York.

Prasad, Om Prakash, (1987). *Aurangzeb*, Khuda Bakhsh Oriental Library, Patna.

Radhakrishnan, S. (1957). *Hindu View of Life*.

Readers Digest Selection (1993). *Inspiring People*, RDI Pub., Mumbai.

Russell, Bertrand (1945). *History of Western Philosophy*, Simon and Schuster, New York.

Sandweiss, Samuel H. (1975). *Sai Baba and Psychiatrist*, Gulab Singh & Sons, New York.

Satsang, R.S. *Philosophy of the Masters*, Beas Satsang, Punjab.

Shashi Bhushan (1986). *Fundamentalism*, National Convention on Secularism, New Delhi.

Sri Aurobindo (1995). *More Light on Yoga*, Sri Aurobindo Ashram, Pondicherry.

Swami Chinmayananda (1991). *The Pursuit of Happiness*, Chinmaya Mission Trust, Mumbai.

Swami Vivekananda (1993). *Karamyoga*, Maitreya Pub., New Delhi.

Tagore, Rabindranath, *Miscellaneous Essays*.

Thoreau, Henry D. (1952). *Nature and Liberty*, Liberal Arts Press, New York.

Titus, Harold H. (1970). *The Range of Philosophy*, Affiliated East West Press, New York.

Ving Tcit Chan (1962). *A Source Book of Chinese Philosophy*, Priceton University Press.

Voltaire (1759) *Candide*.

William Gerber (Ed.) (1967). *The Mind of India*, McMillan Co., New York.

Wily, Brandt, (1980). *North-South*, M.I.T., Boston.

Index